W9-APK-550

FAST TALK

French

lonely planet

Fast Talk French
1st edition – May 2004

Published by
Lonely Planet Publications Pty Ltd ABN 36 005 607 983
90 Maribyrnong St, Footscray, Victoria 3011, Australia

Lonely Planet Offices
Australia Locked Bag 1, Footscray, Victoria 3011
USA 150 Linden St, Oakland CA 94607
UK 72-82 Rosebery Ave, London, EC1R 4RW
France 1 rue du Dahomey, 75011 Paris

Publisher Roz Hopkins
Publishing Manager Peter D'Onghia
Commissioning Editors Karin Vidstrup Monk, Karina Coates
Project Manager Fabrice Rocher
Series Designer Yukiyoshi Kamimura
Layout Designer Patrick Marris
Editors Francesca Coles, Ben Handicott
Also thanks to Michael Janes

Photography
Eiffel Tower, Paris by Jan Stromme
© Lonely Planet Images

ISBN 1 74059 993 4

text © Lonely Planet Publications Pty Ltd 2004

10 9 8 7 6 5 4

Printed by the Bookmaker International Ltd
Printed in China

CHAT 6

EXPLORE 13

SHOP 20

ENJOY 25

EAT & DRINK 27

CONTENTS

3

CONTENTS

Language name: French

French is known to its native speakers as *le français*, ler fron-say

Language family: Romance

French belongs to the Romance family of languages and is a close relative of both Italian and Spanish. It's also quite closely related to English.

Key country & secondary countries:

France is the key French-speaking country but almost 30 countries cite French as an official language, among them Belgium, Luxembourg, Switzerland and the province of Quebec, Canada. France's colonial expansion spread French to countries in Africa, the Pacific and the Caribbean.

Approximate number of speakers:

80 million people speak French as their first language. A further 50 million speak it as their second language.

Donations to English:

Due to an invasion of England in the 11th century, French has contributed widely to the vocabulary of English, so you're sure to recognise many words.

Grammar:

The structure of French holds no major surprises for English speakers as the two languages are quite closely related.

Pronunciation:

The sounds of French can almost all be found in English. The few sounds that do differ from English, including the silent *h* and the throaty *r* will be familiar to most through their contact with French via film and television.

Abbreviations used in this book:

m	masculine	sg	singular	pol	polite
f	feminine	pl	plural	inf	informal

5

CHAT
Meeting & greeting

Hello.	*Bonjour.*	bon·zhoor
Hi.	*Salut.*	sa·lew
Good morning/ afternoon.	*Bonjour.*	bon·zhoor
Good evening/night.	*Bonsoir.*	bon·swar
See you later.	*À bientôt.*	a byun·to
Goodbye.	*Au revoir.*	o rer·vwar
Mr/Sir	*Monsieur (M)*	mer·syer
Ms/Mrs	*Madame (Mme)*	ma·dam
Miss	*Mademoiselle (Mlle)*	mad·mwa·zel
Doctor	*Docteur (Dr)*	dok·ter

How are you?

Comment allez-vous? pol	ko·mon ta·lay·voo
Ça va? inf	sa va

Essentials

Yes.	*Oui.*	wee
No.	*Non.*	non
Please.	*S'il vous plaît.*	seel voo play
Thank you (very much).	*Merci (beaucoup).*	mair·see (bo·koo)
You're welcome.	*Je vous en prie.*	zher voo zon·pree
Excuse me.	*Excusez-moi.*	ek·skew·zay·mwa
Sorry.	*Pardon.*	par·don

Fine. And you?
Bien, merci. — byun mair·see
Et vous/toi? pol/inf — ay voo/twa

What's your name?
Comment vous appelez-vous? pol — ko·mon voo za·play·voo
Comment tu t'appelles? inf — ko·mon tew ta·pel

My name is ...
Je m'appelle ... — zher ma·pel ...

I'd like to introduce you to ...
Je vous présente ... — zher voo pray·zont ...

I'm pleased to meet you.
Enchanté(e). m/f — on·shon·tay

It's been great meeting you.
Ravi d'avoir fait — ra·vee da·vwar fay
votre/ta connaissance. pol/inf — vo·trer/ta ko·nay·sons

This is my ...	*Voici mon/ma ...* m/f	vwa·see mon/ma ...
child	*enfant* m&f	on·fon
colleague	*collègue* m&f	ko·leg
friend	*ami(e)* m/f	a·mee
husband	*mari* m	ma·ree
partner (intimate)	*partenaire* m&f	par·ter·nair
wife	*femme* f	fam

I'm here ...	*Je suis ici ...*	zher swee zee·see ...
for a holiday	*pour les vacances*	poor lay va·kons
on business	*pour le travail*	poor ler tra·vai
to study	*pour les études*	poor lay zay·tewd
with my family	*avec ma famille*	a·vek ma fa·mee·yer
with my partner	*avec mon/ma*	a·vek mon/ma
	partenaire m/f	par·ter·nair

How long are you here for?

Vous êtes ici pour	voo·zet ee·see poor
combien de temps? pol	kom·byun der tom
Tu es ici pour	tew ay zee·see poor
combien de temps? inf	kom·byun der tom

I'm here for ... days/weeks.

Je reste ici ...	zher rest ee·see ...
jours/semaines.	zhoor/ser·men

For numbers, see the box feature in **LOOK UP**, page 67.

Here's my ...	*Voici mon ...*	vwa·see mon ...
What's your ...?	*Quel est votre ...?* pol	kel ay vo·trer ...
	Quel est ton ...? inf	kel ay ton ...
address	*adresse*	a·dress
email address	*e-mail*	ay·mel
fax number	*numéro*	new·may·ro
	de fax	der faks
home number	*numéro de*	new·may·ro der
	téléphone	tay·lay·fon
mobile number	*numéro*	new·may·ro
	de portable	der por·ta·bler
work number	*numéro*	new·may·ro
	au travail	tra·vai

Breaking the language barrier

Do you speak English?

Parlez-vous anglais?	par·lay·voo ong·glay

Does anyone speak English?

Y a-t-il quelqu'un qui	ee·a·teel kel·kung kee
parle anglais?	par long·glay

Do you understand?
Comprenez-vous?   kom·prer·nay·voo

I understand.
Je comprends.   zher kom·pron

I don't understand.
Je ne comprends pas.   zher ner kom·pron pa

I speak a little.
Je parle un peu.   zher parl um per

What does '*ça va*' mean?
Que veut dire 'ça va'?   ker ver deer sa va

How do you ...?	*Comment ...?*	ko·mon ...
pronounce this	*le prononcez-vous*	ler pro·non·say voo
write '*bonjour*'	*est-ce qu'on écrit*	es kon ay·kree
	'bonjour'	bon·zhoor

Could you	*Pourriez-vous ...,*	poo·ree·yay voo ...
please ...?	*s'il vous plaît?*	seel voo play
repeat that	*répéter*	ray·pay·tay
speak more	*parler plus*	par·lay plew
slowly	*lentement*	lon·ter·mon
write it down	*l'écrire*	lay·kreer

Personal details

I'm from ...	*Je viens ...*	zher vyun ...
England	*de l'Angleterre*	der long·gler·tair
Ireland	*de l'Irlande*	der leer·lond
Scotland	*de l'Ecosse*	der lay·kos
the USA	*des États Unis*	day zay·taz ew·nee

Where are you from?

Vous venez d'où? pol		voo ver·nay doo
Tu viens d'où? inf		tew vyun doo

I'm ...	*Je suis ...*	zher swee ...
single	*célibataire*	say·lee·ba·tair
married	*marié(e)* m/f	mar·yay
separated	*séparé(e)* m/f	say·pa·ray
divorced	*divorcé(e)* m/f	dee·vor·say

Occupations & study

I'm a ...	*Je suis*	zher sweez
	un/une ... m/f	un/ewn ...
businessperson	*homme/femme*	om/fem
	d'affaires m/f	da·fair
chef	*cuisinier/*	kwee·zee·nyay/
	cuisinière m/f	kwee·zee·nyair
teacher	*professeur* m&f	pro·fay·ser

I work in ...	*Je travaille dans ...*	zher tra·vai don ...
education	*l'enseignement*	lon·sen·yer·mon
health	*la santé*	la son·tay
sales &	*la vente et le*	la vont ay ler
marketing	*marketing*	mar·kay·teeng

I'm studying ...	*Je fais des*	zher fay day
	études ...	zay·tewd ...
engineering	*d'ingénieur*	dun·zhay·nyer
French	*de français*	der fron·say
media	*des médias*	day may·dya

For other occupations, see the dictionary in **LOOK UP**, page 70.

Age

How old are you? (to an adult)
Quel âge avez-vous?   kel azh a·vay·voo

How old are you? (to a child)
Quel âge as-tu?   kel azh a·tew

How old is your son/daughter?
Quel âge a votre fils/fille?   kel azh a vo·trer fees/fee·yer

I'm ... years old.
J'ai ... ans.   zhay ... on

He/She is ... years old.
Il/Elle a ... ans.   eel/el a ... on

For your age, see the numbers box in **LOOK UP**, page 67.

For your age, see the numbers box in **LOOK UP**, page 67.

Feelings

I'm ...	*J'ai ...*	zhay ...
I'm not ...	*Je n'ai pas ...*	zher nay pa ...
Are you ...?	*Avez-vous ...?* pol	a·vay voo ...
	As-tu ...? inf	a·tew ...
cold	*froid*	frwa
hungry	*faim*	fum
thirsty	*soif*	swaf
I'm ...	*Je suis ...*	zher swee ...
I'm not ...	*Je ne suis pas ...*	zher ner swee pa ...
Are you ...?	*Êtes-vous ...?* pol	et voo ...
	Es-tu ...? inf	ay·tew ...
happy	*content(e)* m/f	kon·ton(t)
sad	*triste*	treest
satisfied	*satisfait(e)* m/f	sa·tees·fay(t)

11

Beliefs

I'm ...	Je suis ...	zher swee ...
I'm not ...	Je ne suis pas ...	zher ner swee pa ...
agnostic	agnostique	ag·no·steek
atheist	athée	a·tay
Buddhist	bouddhiste	boo·deest
Catholic	catholique	ka·to·leek
Christian	chrétien(ne) m/f	kray·tyun/kray·tyen
Hindu	hindou(e) m/f	un·doo
Jewish	juif/juive m/f	zhweef/zhweev
Muslim	musulman(e) m/f	mew·zewl·mon/ mew·zewl·man
practising	pratiquant(e) m/f	pra·tee·kon(t)
Protestant	protestant(e) m/f	pro·tay·ston(t)

Weather

What's the weather like?
Quel temps fait-il? kel tom fay·teel

(Today) It's ...	(Aujourd'hui) Il fait ...	(o·zhoor·dwee) eel fay ...
Will it be ... tomorrow?	Est-ce qu'il fera ... demain?	es·keel fe·ra ... der·mun
(very) cold	(très) froid	(tray) frwa
(very) hot	(très) chaud	(tray) sho

It's cloudy.	Le temps est couvert.	ler tom ay koo·vair
It's raining.	Il pleut.	eel pler
It's sunny.	Il fait beau.	eel fay bo
It's snowing.	Il neige.	eel nezh

EXPLORE
Doing the sights

What would you do if you had just one day?
Que feriez-vous si vous n'aviez   ker fe·ryay voo see voo nav·yay
qu'un jour de disponible?   kun zhoor der dees·pon·ee·bler

Do you have information on local places of interest?
Avez-vous des renseignements   a·vay·voo day ron·sen·yer·mon
sur les endroits à visiter?   sewr lay zon·drwa a vee·zee·tay

I'd like to see ...
J'aimerais voir ...   zhem·ray vwar ...

I have (one day).
J'ai (un jour).   zhay (un zhoor)

What's that?
Qu'est-ce que c'est?   kes·ker say

Who made it?
Qui l'a fait?   kee la fay

How old is it?
Ça date de quand?   sa dat der kon

I'd like a/an ...	*Je voudrais ...*	zher voo·dray ...
audio set	*un écouteur*	un ay·koo·ter
catalogue	*un catalogue*	ung ka·ta·log
city map	*un plan de la ville*	um plon der la veel
guide	*un guide*	ung geed
guidebook	*un guide*	ung geed
(in English)	*(en anglais)*	(on ong·lay)
local map	*une carte*	ewn kart
	de la région	der la ray·zhyon

13

Could you take a photograph of me?
Pouvez-vous me prendre   poo·vay·voo mer pron·drer
en photo?   on fo·to

Can I take photographs?
Je peux prendre des photos?   zher per pron·drer day fo·to

I'll send you the photograph.
Je vous enverrai la photo.   zher voo zon·vay·ray la fo·to

Gallery & museum hopping

When's the ...	... *ouvre à*	... oo·vrer a
open?	*quelle heure?*	kel er
gallery	*La galerie*	la gal·ree
museum	*Le musée*	ler mew·zay

What's in the collection?
Qu'est-ce qu'il y a   kes·keel·ya
dans la collection?   don la ko·lek·syon

It's an exhibition of ...
C'est une exposition de ...   set ewn ek·spo·zee·syon der ...

I like the works of ...
J'aime l'œuvre de ...   zhem ler·vrer der ...

It reminds me of ...
Cela me rappelle ...   ser·la mer ra·pel ...

... **art**	*l'art ...*	lar ...
contemporary	*contemporain*	kon·tom·po·run
impressionist	*impressionniste*	um·pray·syo·neest
modernist	*moderniste*	mo·dair·neest
Renaissance	*de la Renaissance*	der la rer·nay·sons

Getting in

What's the admission charge?
Quel est le prix d'admission?   kel ay ler pree dad·mee·syon

It costs (seven euros).
Ça coûte (sept euros).   sa koot (set er·ro)

What time does it ...?	*Quelle est l'heure ...?*	kel ay ler ...
close	*de fermeture*	der fer·mer·tewr
open	*d'ouverture*	doo·vair·tewr

Is there a discount for ...?	*Il y a une réduction pour les ...?*	eel ya ewn ray·dewk·syon poor lay ...
children	*enfants*	zon·fon
families	*familles*	fa·mee·yer
groups	*groupes*	groop
pensioners	*personnes du troisième âge*	pair·son dew trwa·zyem azh
students	*étudiants*	zay·tew·dyon

Tours

Can you recommend a ...?	*Pouvez-vous me recommander une ...?*	poo·vay·voo mer rer·ko·mon·day ewn ...
boat trip	*excursion en bateau*	eks·kewr·syon en ba·to
day trip	*excursion d'une journée*	eks·koor·syon dewn zhoor·nay
tour	*excursion*	eks·kewr·syon

When's the next ...?	C'est quand la prochaine ...?	say kon la pro·shen ...
boat trip	excursion en bateau	eks·kewr·syon en ba·to
day trip	excursion d'une journée	eks·koor·syon dewn zhoor·nay
tour	excursion	eks·koor·syon
Is ... included?	Est-ce que ... est inclus(e)? m/f	es·ker ... ay tung·klew(z)
accommodation	le logement m	ler lozh·mon
the admission charge	le prix m d'entrée	ler pree don·tray
food	la nourriture f	la noo·ree·tewr
transport	le transport m	ler trons·por

Do I need to take ...?
Dois-je prendre ...? — dwa·zher pron·drer ...

The guide will pay.
Le guide va payer. — ler geed va pay·yay

The guide has paid.
Le guide a payé. — ler geed a pay·yay

How long is the tour?
L'excursion dure combien de temps? — leks·kewr·syon dewr kom·byun der tom

What time should we be back?
On doit rentrer pour quelle heure? — on dwa ron·tray poor kel er

I'm with them.
Je suis avec eux. — zher swee za·vek er

I've lost my group.
J'ai perdu mon groupe. — zhay pair·dew mon groop

Have you seen a group of (Australians)?
Avez-vous vu un groupe (d'Australiens)? — a·vay voo vew un groop (dos·tra·lyun)

Top 5 day trips from Paris

If the pace of Paris becomes overwhelming, join the Parisians in escaping to some of these out-of-town oases:

Château de Fontainebleau
sha·to der fon·ten·blo

Surrounded by beautiful gardens, the Château de Fontainebleau is one of the most charmingly decorated and furnished châteaux in France. Strolling in the adjacent woods is a favourite Parisian pastime.

Cathédrale de Chartres
ka·tay·dral der shar·trer

A magnificent medieval cathedral renowned for its Gothic and Romanesque spires, ornamental portals and awe-inspiring stained-glass windows.

Disneyland Paris
dees·nay·lond pa·ree

The most popular fee-paying attraction in Europe, it comprises an amusement park, Disney Studios and Disneyland village, featuring restaurants, bars and even a skating rink.

Musée de Claude Monet à Giverny
mew·say der clod mo·nay a zhee·ver·nee

The home of impressionist Claude Monet from 1883–1926 in the delightful village of Giverny. The gardens surrounding the house provided the inspiration for some of Monet's most famous paintings, including the *Water Lilies* series.

Versailles
ver·sai

The site of the grandest and most famous château in France, Versailles was the kingdom's political capital and the seat of the royal court for more than a century, until the Revolution in 1789. The château is also famous for its splendid ornamental gardens and fountains.

Top 10 Paris sights

It would take a lifetime to unearth all the riches that Paris has to offer. If you don't have that much time on your hands, make sure you pack in a few of these famous highlights:

Arc de Triomphe   ark der tree·omf
Commissioned by Napoleon, the Arc de Triomphe towers 50m above Place Charles de Gaulle, the vast traffic roundabout from which 12 boulevards, including the Champs Élysées, radiate.

Centre Pompidou   son·trer pom·pee·doo
The Pompidou Centre has amazed and delighted visitors since it was built in the mid-1970s — not just for its outstanding collection of modern art, but for its radical, colourful 'inside out' architectural statement.

Cimetière du Père Lachaise   seem·tyer dew pair la·shayz
Père Lachaise is the most visited necropolis in the world. Many famous people are buried here, including the composer Chopin, singer Edith Piaf, rock star Jim Morrison, dancer Isadora Duncan, the writers Molière, Oscar Wilde and Marcel Proust, and the artists Delacroix and Modigliani.

Jardin du Luxembourg   zhar·dun dew look·som·boor
This 25-hectare park with its Franco-Italian style terraces, floral displays and chestnut groves is a favourite Parisian fair-weather playground. Children can enjoy the boating pond, puppet theatre, pony rides and carousel.

Montmartre   mon·mar·trer
Montmartre is crowned by the wedding-cake-like church *Basilique du Sacré Cœur*, one of Paris' most recognisable landmarks. Despite the throngs of tourists, Montmartre retains a bohemian village feel with its narrow twisting cobblestone streets, buskers and street artists.

Musée d'Orsay
mew·zay dor·say

Once a train station, the *Musée d'Orsay* now houses under its vault a superb collection of French Impressionist and Post-Impressionist works. On display are France's national collection of paintings, sculptures, *objets d'art* and other works, including those by Rodin, Renoir and Van Gogh.

Musée du Louvre
mew·zay dew loo·vrer

The Louvre is arguably the world's greatest art museum but despite its overwhelming richness many would-be visitors are daunted by its sheer size. An enjoyable way to sample its great works is to buy a map-guide to direct you to the works you really want to see.

Musée Rodin
mew·zay ro·dun

One of the most tranquil spots in the city, this is also many visitors' favourite Paris museum. A huge body of the vital sculptor's works are housed inside his magnificent 18th-century residence and in the surrounding rose garden.

Notre Dame
no·trer dam

The cathedral of Notre Dame, built between 1163 and 1345, is a masterpiece of French Gothic architecture. It has also been Catholic Paris' ceremonial focus for seven centuries. The building is remarkable for its sublime balance, and its immense interior is a marvel of medieval engineering.

Tour Eiffel
toor e·fel

Named for its designer Gustave Eiffel, this icon of mass tourism reaches a height of 320m. Even the most jaded visitor will feel a frisson of excitement as they ascend through the girders, and the panoramic views from any of the three levels are breathtaking. At night, transformed by clever illumination, it floats as though built of nothing more substantial than filaments of light.

EXPLORE

SHOP
Essentials

Where's ...? *Où est-ce qu'il y a ...?* oo es·keel ya ...
- **a bank** *une banque* ewn bongk
- **a cake shop** *une pâtisserie* ewn pa·tees·ree
- **a grocery store** *une épicerie* ewn ay·pee·sree

Where can I buy ...?
Où puis-je acheter ...? oo pweezh ash·tay ...

I'd like to buy ...
Je voudrais acheter ... zher voo·dray ash·tay ...

Do you have any others?
Vous en avez d'autres? voo zon a·vay do·trer

Can I look at it?
Est-ce que je peux le/la voir? m/f es·ker zher per ler/la vwar

I'm just looking.
Je regarde. zher rer·gard

Could I have it wrapped?
Pouvez-vous l'envelopper? poo·vay·voo lon·vlo·pay

Could I have a bag, please?
Puis-je avoir un sac, s'il vous plaît? pweezh a·vwar un sak seel voo play

Does it have a guarantee?
Est-ce qu'il y a une garantie? es keel ya ewn ga·ron·tee

Can I have it sent overseas?
Pouvez-vous me poo·vay·voo mer
l'envoyer à l'étranger? lon·vwa·yay a lay·tron·zhay

Can I pick it up later?
Je peux passer le/la zher per pa·say ler/la
prendre plus tard? m/f pron·drer plew tar

It's faulty/broken.
C'est défectueux/cassé. say day·fek·twer/ka·say

I'd like ..., please. *Je voudrais ...,* zher voo·dray ...
  s'il vous plaît. seel voo play
  a discount *un rabais* un ra·bay
  my money back *un remboursement* un rom·boors·mon
  to change this *échanger ceci* ay·shonzh·ay ser·see
  to return this *rapporter ceci* ra·por·tay ser·see

Paying

How much is it?
Ça fait combien? sa fay kom·byun

Can you write down the price?
Pourriez-vous écrire le prix? poo·ryay·voo ay·kreer ler pree

Can I have smaller notes?
Pourriez-vous me donner des poo·ryay voo mer do·nay day
petites coupures? per·teet koo·pewr

Do you accept ...? *Est-ce que je* es·ker zher
  peux payer avec ...? per pay·yay a·vek ...
  credit cards *une carte* ewn kart
  de crédit der kray·dee
  debit cards *une carte* ewn kart
  de débit der day·bee
  travellers *des chèques* day shek
  cheques *de voyages* der vwa·yazh

I'd like ... *Je voudrais ...* zher voo·dray ...
  a receipt *un reçu* un rer·sew
  my change *ma monnaie* ma mo·nay

That's too expensive.
C'est trop cher. say tro shair

Do you have something cheaper?
Avez-vous quelque a·vay·voo kel·ker
chose de moins cher? shoz der mwun shair

Clothes & shoes

I'm looking for ...	*Je cherche ...*	zher shairsh ...
jeans	*un jean*	un zheen
shoes	*des chaussures*	day sho·sewr
underwear	*des sous-vêtements*	day soo·vet·mon

Can I try it on?
Puis-je l'essayer? pwee·zher lay·say·yay

Hot Paris shop spots

Paris is the home of chic and a sublime place to shop. Avid consumers and window-shoppers alike can sate their appetites at the following locales:

Abbesses (18e) – vintage clothing • streetwear • fabrics • music
Marais (3e) – hip boutiques • books • music • homewares • quirky speciality stores
Opéra (9e) – major department stores • clothing • perfume • cosmetics
Place Vendôme (1er) – jewellery • luxury goods
Quartier Latin (5e) – books • stationery
Rue de Paradis (10e) – glass • crystal • china • Limoges wear
Rue de Rivoli & Les Halles (1er & 2e) – international brands • clothes • shoes • books • music • toys • perfume
St-Germain (6e) – designer clothes & accessories • shoes • antiques • speciality stores

My size is (42).
Je fais du (quarante-deux). zher fay dew (ka·ront·der)

Do you have this in size (36)?
Vous avez la même voo za·vay la mem
chose en taille (trente-six)? shoz on tai (tront·sees)

It doesn't fit.
Ce n'est pas la bonne taille. ser nay pa la bon tai

small	*petit*	per·tee
medium	*moyen*	mwai·un
large	*large*	larzh

Books & music

Is there an English-language bookshop?
Y a-t-il une librairie de ya·teel ewn lee·brair·ee der
langue anglaise? long ong·glayz

Is there an English-language section?
Y a-t-il un rayon anglais? ya·teel un ray·yon ong·glay

Do you have a/an	*Avez-vous . . .*	a·vay·voo . . .
. . . in English?	*en anglais?*	on ong·glay
novel by . . .	*un roman de . . .*	un ro·mon der . . .
entertainment	*un guide des*	ung geed day
guide	*spectacles*	spek·ta·kler
I'd like a . . .	*Je voudrais . . .*	zher voo·dray . . .
map (city)	*un plan de la ville*	um plon der la veel
map (road)	*une carte routière*	ewn kart roo·tyair
newspaper	*un journal*	un zhoor·nal
(in English)	*(en anglais)*	(on ong·glay)
pen	*un stylo*	un stee·lo
postcard	*une carte postale*	ewn kart pos·tal

I'd like (a) ...	Je voudrais ...	zher voo·dray ...
blank CD	un CD vierge	un say·day vyerzh
CD	un CD	un say·day
headphones	un casque	ung kask

I'm looking for a CD by ...
Je cherche un CD de ... — zher shairsh un say·day der ...

What's his/her best recording?
Quel est son meilleur enregistrement? — kel ay som may·yer on·rer·zhees·trer·mon

Can I listen to it here?
Je peux l'écouter ici? — zher per lay·koo·tay ee·see

Photography

I need ...	J'ai besoin d'une	zhay ber·zwun dewn
film for this camera.	pellicule ... pour cet appareil.	pay·lee·kewl ... poor say ta·pa·ray
APS	APS	a·pay·es
B&W	en noir et blanc	on nwar ay blong
colour	couleur	koo·ler
(100) ASA	(cent) ASA	(son) a es a

Can you ...?	Pouvez-vous ...?	poo·vay·voo ...
develop	développer	day·vlo·pay
this film	cette pellicule	set pay·lee·kewl
load my	charger ma	shar·zhay ma
film	pellicule	pay·lee·kewl

How much is it to develop this film?
C'est combien pour développer cette pellicule? — say kom·byun poor day·vlo·pay set pay·lee·kewl

When will it be ready?
Quand est-ce que cela sera prêt? — kon tes·ker ser·la ser·ra pray

ENJOY
What's on?

What's on ...?	Qu'est-ce qu'on joue ...?	kes·kon zhoo ...
locally	dans le coin	don ler kwun
this weekend	ce week-end	ser week·end
today	aujourd'hui	o·zhoor·dwee
tonight	ce soir	ser swar

Where are the ...?	Où sont les ...?	oo son lay ...
clubs	clubs	klerb
discos	discothèques	dees·ko·tek
gay hangouts	boîtes gaies	bwat gay
places to eat	restaurants	res·to·ron
pubs	pubs	perb

Is there a local ... guide?	Y a-t-il un programme ...?	ya·teel un pro·gram ...
entertainment	des spectacles	day spek·ta·kler
film	des films	day feelm

I'd like to go to a/the ...	Je voudrais aller ...	zher voo·dray a·lay ...
ballet	au ballet	o ba·lay
bar	au bar	o bar
café	au café	o ka·fay
cinema	au cinéma	o see·nay·ma
concert	à un concert	a ung kon·sair
nightclub	en boîte	on bwat
opera	à l'opéra	a lo·pay·ra
restaurant	au restaurant	o res·to·ron
theatre	au théâtre	o tay·a·trer

Meeting up

What time shall we meet?
On se retrouve à quelle heure?   on ser rer·troov a kel er

Where will we meet?
On se retrouve où?   on ser rer·troov oo

I'll pick you up at (seven).
Je viendrais te chercher   zher vyun·dray te shair·shay
à (sept heures).   a (set er)

Let's meet at ...	*On peut se retrouver ...*	on per ser rer·troo·vay ...
(eight o'clock)	*à (huit heures)*	a (wee ter)
the (entrance)	*devant (l'entrée)*	der·von (lon·tray)

Small talk

What do you do in your spare time?
Que fais-tu pendant tes loisirs?   ker fay·tew pon·don tay lwa·zeer

Do you like ...?	*Aimez-vous/*	em·ez voo/
	Aimes-tu ...? pol/inf	em·tew ...
I like ...	*J'aime ...*	zhem ...
I don't like ...	*Je n'aime pas ...*	zher nem pa ...
dancing	*danser*	don·say
going to concerts	*aller aux concerts*	a·lay o kon·sair
going to	*aller au*	a·lay o
the theatre	*théâtre*	tay·a·trer

I like ...	*J'aime les ...*	zhem lay...
I don't like ...	*Je n'aime pas les ...*	zher nem pa lay ...
action movies	*films d'action*	feelm dak·syon
French films	*films français*	feelm fron·say
sci-fi films	*films de*	feelm der
	science-fiction	syons feek·syon

EAT & DRINK

breakfast	petit-déjeuner m	per·tee day·zher·nay
lunch	déjeuner m	day·zher·nay
dinner	dîner m	dee·nay
snack	casse-croûte m	kas·kroot

Choosing & booking

Where would you go for a celebration?
On va où pour faire la fête?   on va oo poor fair la fet

Can you recommend a ...?	Est-ce que vous pouvez me conseiller ...?	es·ker voo poo·vay mer kon·say·yay ...
bar	un bar	um bar
café	un café	ung ka·fay
restaurant	un restaurant	un res·to·ron

Where would you go for ...?	Où est-ce qu'on trouve ...?	oo es kon troov ...
a cheap meal	les restaurants bon marché	lay res·to·ron bom mar·shay
fine dining	un bon restaurant	un bon res·to·ron
local specialities	les spécialités locales	lay spay·sya·lee·tay lo·kal

I'd like ..., please.	Je voudrais ..., s'il vous plaît.	zher voo·dray ... seel voo play
a table for (five)	une table pour (cinq) personnes	ewn ta·bler poor (sungk) pair·son
smoking/ nonsmoking	pour fumeurs/ non-fumeurs	poor few·mer/ non·few·mer

27

Eateries

Sampling and savouring French cuisine is one of the great joys of a visit to France. Give free rein to your gastronomic curiosity at these establishments:

auberge   o·bairzh
serves traditional country fare in a relaxed atmosphere

bistro   bees·tro
can be anything from a pub with inexpensive snacks to a bar with a fully fledged restaurant menu

brasserie   bras·ree
serves inexpensive full meals, drinks and coffee from early in the morning to late at night

café   ka·fay
an important focal point for social life and, in addition to coffee, it sells basic food including baguette sandwiches

cafétéria   ka·fay·tay·ree·a
offers a good selection of cheap dishes you can select and pay for at a counter

crêperie   krep·ree
specialises in *crêpes* (thin pancakes) which are folded or rolled over a filling

relais routier   re·lay roo·tyay
a truck stop café — these places provide a hearty break and are not as rough and ready as the UK or US equivalent

restaurant   res·to·ron
typically specialises in a particular cuisine and is usually open only at set times for lunch and dinner

restaurant libre-service   res·to·ronlee·brer ser·vees
a self-service restaurant similar to a *cafétéria*

salon de thé   sa·lon der tay
a trendy and pricey establishment that serves sweet and savoury pastries and salads, in addition to tea and coffee

Ordering

What would you recommend?
Qu'est-ce que vous conseillez?   kes·ker voo kon·say·yay

I'd like ..., please.	*Je voudrais ..., s'il vous plaît.*	zher voo·dray ... seel voo play
the bill	*l'addition*	la·dee·syon
the chicken	*le poulet*	ler poo·lay
the menu	*la carte*	la kart
a napkin	*une serviette*	ewn sair·vyet
pepper	*le poivre*	ler pwa·vrer
salt	*le sel*	ler sel
the set menu	*le menu du jour*	ler mer·new dew zhoor
the wine list	*la carte des vins*	la kart day vun

I'd like it ...	*J'aime ça ...*	zhem sa ...
medium	*à point*	a pwun
rare	*saignant*	say·nyon
well-done	*bien cuit*	byun kwee
with the dressing on the side	*avec la sauce à côté*	a·vek la sos a ko·tay

Nonalcoholic drinks

(cup of) coffee	*(un) café* m	(ung) ka·fay
(cup of) tea	*(un) thé* m	(un) tay
black ...	*... noir*	... nwar
... with milk	*... au lait*	... o lay
... without/ with sugar	*... sans/avec sucre*	... son/a·vek sew·krer
orange juice	*jus* m *d'orange*	zhew do·ronzh
soft drink	*boisson* f *non-alcoolisée*	bwa·son non·al·ko·lee·zay

... water	*eau* f ...	o ...
hot	*chaude*	shod
sparkling	*minérale*	mee·nay·ral
mineral	*gazeuse*	ga·zerz
still mineral	*minérale*	mee·nay·ral
	non-gazeuse	nong·ga·zerz

Alcoholic drinks

beer	*bière* f	byair
brandy	*cognac* m	ko·nyak
champagne	*champagne* m	shom·pan·yer
cocktail	*cocktail* m	kok·tel

a bottle of ... wine	*une bouteille de vin* ...	ewn boo·tay der vun ...
a glass of ... wine	*un verre de vin* ...	un vair der vun ...
red	*rouge*	roozh
sparkling	*mousseux*	moo·ser
white	*blanc*	blong

a ... of beer	*... de bière*	... der byair
bottle	*une bouteille*	ewn boo·tay
glass	*un verre*	un vair

a shot of	*un petit verre*	um per·tee vair
(whisky)	*de (whisky)*	der (wees·kee)

In the bar

I'll have (a gin).
  Je prends (un gin).   zher pron (un zheen)

Same again, please.
  La même chose, s'il vous plaît.   la mem shoz seel voo play

I'll buy you a drink.
Je vous offre un verre.   zher voo zo·frer un vair

What would you like?
Qu'est-ce que vous voulez?   kes·ker voo voo·lay

It's my round.
C'est ma tournée.   say ma toor·nay

Cheers!
Santé!   son·tay

Buying food

What's the local speciality?
Quelle est la   kel ay la
spécialité locale?   spay·sya·lee·tay lo·kal

What's that?
Qu'est ce que c'est?   kes ker say

How much?
Combien?   kom·byun

How much is (a kilo)?
C'est combien pour   say kom·byun poor
(un kilo)?   (un kee·lo)

I'd like ...	*Je voudrais ...*	zher voo·dray ...
(200) grams	*(deux cents) grammes*	(der son) gram
(two) kilos	*(deux) kilos*	(der) kee·lo
(three) pieces	*(trois) morceaux*	(trwa) mor·so
(six) slices	*(six) tranches*	(see) tronsh
some of that/ those	*de ça*	der sa

cooked	*cuit(e)* m/f	kwee(t)
dried	*sec/sèche* m/f	sek/sesh
fresh	*frais/fraîche* m/f	fray/fresh
frozen	*surgelé(e)* m/f	sewr·zher·lay

Enough, thanks.	*Ça ira, merci.*	sa ee·ra mair·see
A bit more, please.	*Encore un peu, s'il vous plaît.*	ong·kor un per seel voo play
Less, thanks.	*Moins, s'il vous plaît.*	mwun seel voo play

Special diets & allergies

Is there a (vegetarian) restaurant near here?
| *Y a-t-il un restaurant (végétarien) par ici?* | ya·teel un res·to·ron (vay·zhay·ta·ryun) par ee·see |

Do you have (vegetarian) food?
| *Vous faites les repas (végétariens)?* | voo fet lay rer·pa (vay·zhay·ta·ryun) |

Could you prepare a meal without ...?	*Pouvez-vous préparer un repas sans ...?*	poo·vay·voo pray·pa·ray un rer·pa son ...
butter	*du beurre*	dew ber
eggs	*des œufs*	day zer
meat stock	*du bouillon gras*	dew boo·yon gra

I'm ...	*Je suis ...*	zher swee ...
vegan	*végétalien(ne)* m/f	vay·zhay·ta·lyun/ vay·zhay·ta·lyen
vegetarian	*végétarien(ne)* m/f	vay·zhay·ta·ryun/ vay·zhay·ta·ryen

I'm allergic to ...	Je suis allergique ...	zher swee za·lair·zheek ...
caffeine	à la caféine	a la ka·fay·een
dairy produce	aux produits laitiers	o pro·dwee lay·tyay
eggs	aux œufs	o zer
gluten	au gluten	o glew·ten
nuts	aux noix	o nwa
seafood	aux fruits de mer	o frwee der mair

I don't eat/drink ...
Je ne mange/bois pas ...   zher ner monzh/bwa pa ...

For more on allergies, see **HELP**, page 66 and **LOOK UP**, page 70.

On the menu

Amuse-gueules	a·mewz·gerl	appetisers
Soupes	soop	soups
Entrées	on·tray	entrees
Salades	sa·lad	salads
Plats Principaux	pla prun·see·po	main courses
Desserts	day·sair	desserts
Boissons	bwa·son	drinks
Apéritifs	a·pay·ree·teef	aperitifs
Spiritueux	spee·ree·tew·er	spirits
Bières	byair	beers
Vins Mousseux	vun moo·ser	sparkling wines
Vins Blancs	vun blong	white wines
Vins Rouges	vun roozh	red wines
Vins de Dessert	vun der day·sair	dessert wines

For more help reading the menu, see the **Menu decoder**, page 34.

Menu decoder

à la vapeur	a la va·per	steamed
abricot m	ab·ree·ko	apricot
agneau m	a·nyo	lamb
agneau m *de lait*	a·nyo de lay	baby lamb
ail m	ai	garlic
aloyau m	a·lwa·yo	sirloin
amandes f pl	a·mond	almonds
ananas m	a·na·nas	pineapple
anchois m	on·shwa	anchovies
andouille f	on·doo·yer	sausage made of intestines
aneth m	a·net	dill
anguille f	ong·gee·yer	eel
artichaut m	ar·tee·sho	artichoke
asperges f	a·spairzh	asparagus
au poivre	o pwa·vrer	with pepper sauce
aubergine f	o·bair·zheen	aubergine • eggplant
avec	a·vek	with
avocat m	a·vo·ka	avocado
banane f	ba·nan	banana
bar m	bar	bass
beignet m	be·nyay	fritter
betterave f	be·trav	beetroot
bifteck m	beef·tek	beefsteak
bisque f	beesk	shellfish soup
bœuf m	berf	beef
bœuf m *bourguignon*	berf boor·geen·yon	beef stew with onions & mushrooms in a burgundy sauce
bouillabaisse f	bwee·a·bes	fish soup from Marseille
bouilli(e) m/f	boo·yee	boiled

bouillon m	boo·yon	broth
bourride f	boo·reed	Provençal white fish soup
braisé(e) m/f	bre·se	braised
brème f	brem	bream
brochet m	bro·shay	pike
cacahuètes f pl	ka·ka·wet	peanuts
caille f	kai·yer	quail
calmar m	kal·mar	squid
canard m	ka·nar	duck
canard m *sauvage*	ka·nar so·vazh	wild duck
caneton m	kan·ton	duckling
carbonnade f	kar·bo·nad	selection of chargrilled meats
carottes f pl	ka·rot	carrots
carrelet m	ka·re·lay	plaice
cassis m	ka·sees	blackcurrant
céleri m	sayl·ree	celery
cerfeuil m	ser·fer·yee	chervil
cerises f pl	se·rees	cherries
cervelle f	ser·vel	brains
champignons m pl	shom·pee·nyon	mushrooms
châtaignes f pl	sha·tayn·nyer	chestnuts
chevreuil m	sher·vrer·yer	venison
chou m	shoo	cabbage
chou-fleur m	shoo·fler	cauliflower
choucroute f	shoo·kroot	pickled cabbage • sauerkraut
ciboulette f	see·boo·let	chives
citron m	see·tron	lemon
citrouille f	see·troo·yer	pumpkin
cochon m *de lait*	ko·shon de lay	suckling pig
concombre m	kon·kom·brer	cucumber
consommé m	kon·so·may	clear soup

contre-filet m	kon·trer fee·lay	sirloin (steak)
coq m *au vin*	kok o vun	chicken cooked with wine, onions & mushrooms
coquilles Saint-Jacques f pl	ko·kee·yer sun zhak	scallops
cornichon m	kor·nee·shon	gherkin
côtelette f	ko·te·let	cutlet
coulis m	koo·lee	purée, usually of fruit or vegetable
courgette f	koor·zhet	courgette • zucchini
crevettes f pl *grises*	kre·vet grees	shrimps
crevettes f pl *roses*	kre·vet ros	prawns
cru(e) m/f	krew	raw
crudités m pl	krew·dee·tay	raw vegetables with dressings
cuisses f pl *de grenouilles*	kwees de grer·noo·yer	frogs legs
cuit(e) m/f	kwee(t)	cooked
cuit(e) m/f *au four*	kwee(t) o foor	baked
darne f	darn	fish cutlet
datte f	dat	date
daurade f	do·rad	sea bream
dinde f	dund	turkey
dindon m	dun·don	turkey
dindonneau m	dun·do·no	young turkey
doux/douce m/f	doo/doos	mild • sweet
du jour	dew zhoor	of the day
écrevisses f pl	e·kre·vees	crayfish
émincé(e) m/f	ay·mun·say	thinly sliced
entrecôte f	on·tre·kot	ribsteak
épaule f	ay·pol	shoulder
épinards m pl	ay·pee·nar	spinach

escargots m pl	es·kar·go	snails
estouffade f	es·too·fad	stew
estragon m	es·tra·gon	tarragon
faisan m	fay·zan	pheasant
fait(e) m/f **à la maison**	fay(t) a la may·son	homemade
farci(e) m/f	far·see	stuffed
fenouil m	fer·noo·yer	fennel
figue f	feeg	fig
filet m	fee·lay	fillet
flamiche f	fla·meesh	leek quiche
foie m	fwa	liver
fraises f pl	frez	strawberries
framboises f pl	from·bwaz	raspberries
fromage m	fro·mazh	cheese
fricassée f	free·ka·say	stewed meat & vegetables in creamy sauce
fumé(e) m/f	few·may	smoked
gambas f pl	gam·bas	king prawns
garniture f	gar·nee·tewr	garnish
gelée f	zhe·lay	jelly
gibier m	zheeb·yay	game
gigot m	zhee·go	leg
grillade f	gree·yad	mixed grill
grillé(e) m/f	gree·yay	grilled
groseilles f pl	gro·zay·yer	gooseberries
hachis m	a·shee	hash (chopped mince meat or vegetables)
haricots m pl **verts**	a·ree·ko ver	French or string beans
homard m	o·mar	lobster
huîtres m pl	wee·trer	oysters
jambon m	zhom·bon	ham
laitance m	lay·tons	roe
laitue f	lay·tew	lettuce

langoustines f pl	long·goo·steen	scampi or Dublin Bay prawns
langue f	long	tongue
lapin m	la·pun	rabbit
lard m	lar	bacon
laurier m	lo·ryay	bay leaf
légumes m pl	lay·gewm	vegetables
lentilles f pl	lon·tee·yer	lentils
lièvre f	lye·vrer	hare
longe f	lonzh	loin
lotte f	lot	monkfish
loup m *de mer*	loo de mer	bass
maison f	may·son	of the house
mange-tout m	monzh·too	sugar peas • snowpeas
maquereau m	ma·kro	mackerel
mariné(e) m/f	ma·ree·nay	marinated
marjolaine f	mar·zho·len	marjoram
marrons m pl	ma·ron	chestnuts
menthe f	mont	mint
menu m *dégustation*	mer·new day·gew·sta·syon	tasting menu
merguez f	mair·gez	spicy red sausage
merlan m	mer·lon	whiting
mirabelle f	mee·ra·bel	plum
moelle f	mwal	marrow
moules f pl	mool	mussels
moules f pl *marinières*	mool ma·ree·nyair	mussels with shallots in white-wine sauce
moutarde f	moo·tard	mustard
mûres f pl	mewr	blackberries
noisettes f pl	nwa·zet	hazelnuts
noix f	nwa	nuts • walnuts
noix f *de coco*	nwa de ko·ko	coconut
oie f	wa	goose

oignon m	o·nyon	onion
olives f pl	o·leev	olives
orange f	o·ronzh	orange
palourdes f pl	poo·lard	clams
pamplemousse m	pom·ple·moos	grapefruit
pané(e) m/f	pa·nay	crumbed
pastèque f	pas·tek	watermelon
patate f *douce*	pa·tat doos	sweet potato
pâté m	pa·tay	paté · pie
pâtes f pl	pat	pasta
pêche f	pesh	peach
persil m	per·see	parsley
petits pois m pl	per·tee pwa	peas
piquant m	pee·kon	spicy hot
pistou m	pees·too	pesto
poché(e) m/f	po·shay	poached
poêle f	pwal	frying pan
poêlé(e) m/f	pwa·lay	pan-fried
poire f	pwar	pear
poireau m	pwa·ro	leek
pois chiches m pl	pwa sheesh	chickpeas
poisson m	pwa·son	fish
poitrine f *de porc*	pwa·treen de por	pork belly
poitrine f *de veau*	pwa·treen de vo	breast of veal
poivre m	pwa·vrer	pepper
poivron m	pwa·vron	capsicum · pepper
pomme f	pom	apple
pomme f *de terre*	pom der tair	potato
porc f	por	pork
potage m	po·tazh	thick soup, usually vegetable
potiron m	po·tee·ron	pumpkin
poularde f	poo·lard	fatted chicken
poulet m	poo·lay	chicken

poulpe m	poolp	octopus
prune f	prewn	plum
pruneau m	prew·no	prune
queue f *de bœuf*	ker de berf	oxtail
radis m	ra·dee	radish
ragoût m	ra·goo	stew of meat or poultry & vegetables
raifort m	ray·for	horseradish
raisins m pl	ray·sun	grapes
ratatouille f	ra·ta·too·yer	eggplant, zucchini, tomato & garlic dish
rillettes f pl	ree·yet	potted meat (pork or goose)
riz m	ree	rice
rognons m pl	ro·nyon	kidneys
romarin m	ro·ma·run	rosemary
rôti(e) m/f	ro·tee	roast
saint-pierre m	sun·pyair	John Dory (fish)
sanglier m	song·glee·yay	wild boar
sardines f pl	sar·deen	sardines
sauge f	sozh	sage
saumon m	so·mon	salmon
séché(e) m/f	se·shay	dried
sel m	sel	salt
selle f	sel	saddle (of meat)
steak m *frites*	stek freet	steak with chips
steak m *tartare*	stek tar·tar	raw minced beef, raw onion & egg yolk
thon m	ton	tuna
thym m	tun	thyme
topinambours m pl	to·pee·nam·boor	Jerusalem artichokes
tournedos m	toor·ne·do	thick slices of fillet
tourte f	toort	pie
tranché(e) m/f	tran·shay	sliced
tripes f pl	treep	tripe

truffes f pl	trewf	truffles
truite f	trweet	trout
veau m	vo	veal
venaison f	ver·nay·son	venison
vinaigre m	vee·nay·grer	vinegar
viande f	vyond	meat
volaille f	vo·lai	poultry

Top eats on the go

If you're out and about and hunger strikes unheralded, join the French in sampling some of these hasty, tasty treats:

baguette sandwich   ba·get son·dweech
crispy bread stick sliced open and filled

choucroute   shoo·kroot
sauerkraut — a variation is *choucroute garnie* sauerkraut served with assorted fresh and smoked meats and sausages

crêpes   krep
large, paper-thin pancakes served with various fillings

croque madame   krok ma·dam
grilled or pan-fried ham and cheese sandwich with a fried egg on top

croque monsieur   krok mer·syer
same as a *croque madame* but without the egg

moules et frites   mool ay freet
mussels served with chips or French fries

pain au chocolat   pun o sho·ko·la
flat croissant with chocolate filling

plat cuisiné   pla kwee·see·nay
pre-prepared meal from a *traiteur* (delicatessen)

steak frites   stek freet
minute steak with chips or French fries

SERVICES
Post office

I want to send a ...	Je voudrais envoyer ...	zher voo·dray on·vwa·yay ...
fax	un fax	un faks
letter	une lettre	ewn le·trer
parcel	un colis	ung ko·lee
postcard	une carte postale	ewn kart pos·tal
I want to buy ...	Je voudrais acheter ...	zher voo·dray ash·tay ...
an envelope	une enveloppe	ewn on·vlop
stamps	des timbres	day tum·brer
Please send it (to Australia) by ...	Envoyez-le (en Australie) ..., s'il vous plaît.	on·vwa·yay·ler (on os·tra·lee) ... seel voo play
airmail	par avion	par a·vyon
express post	en exprès	on neks·pres
regular post	en courrier normal	on koor·yay nor·mal
surface mail	par voie de terre	par vwa der tair

Bank

Where's the nearest ...?	Où est ... le plus proche?	oo ay ... ler plew prosh
automatic teller machine	le guichet automatique de banque	ler gee·shay o·to·ma·teek der bongk
foreign exchange office	le bureau de change	ler bew·ro der shonzh

42

What time does the bank open?
À quelle heure ouvre la banque?   a kel er oo·vrer la bongk

I'd like to ...	*Je voudrais ...*	zher voo·dray ...
Where can I ...?	*Où est-ce que*	oo es·ker
	je peux ...?	zher per ...
arrange a transfer	*faire un virement*	fair un veer·mon
cash a cheque	*encaisser un chèque*	on·kay·say un shek
change a	*changer des*	shon·zhay day
travellers cheque	*chèques de voyage*	shek der vwa·yazh
change	*changer de*	shon·zhay der
money	*l'argent*	lar·zhon
get a cash	*une avance*	ewn a·vons
advance	*de crédit*	der kray·dee
withdraw money	*retirer de*	rer·tee·ray der
	l'argent	lar·zhon

What's the ...?	*Quel est ...?*	kel ay ...
charge	*le tarif*	ler ta·reef
commission	*la commission*	la ko·mee·syon
exchange rate	*le taux de change*	ler to der shonzh

Phone

What's your phone number?
Quel est votre numéro   kel ay vo·trer new·may·ro
de téléphone?   der tay·lay·fon

Where's the nearest public phone?
Où est le téléphone   oo ay ler tay·lay·fon
public le plus proche?   pewb·leek ler plew prosh

I'd like to buy a phone card.
Je voudrais acheter   zher voo·dray ash·tay
une carte téléphonique.   ewn kart tay·lay·fo·neek

43

The number is ...		
Le numéro est ...		ler new·may·ro ay ...
I want to make a ...	*Je veux faire ...*	zher ver fair ...
call	*un appel*	un a·pel
	téléphonique	tay·lay·fo·neek
local call	*un appel local*	un a·pel lo·kal
reverse-charge/	*un appel*	un a·pel
collect call	*en PCV*	on pay say vay
How much	*Quel est le prix ...?*	kel ay ler pree ...
does ... cost?		
a (three)-minute	*d'une*	dewn
call	*communication*	ko·mew·nee·ka·syon
	de (trois) minutes	der (trwa) mee·newt
each extra	*de chaque minute*	der shak mee·newt
minute	*supplémentaire*	sew·play·mon·tair

Mobile/cell phone

What are the rates?
Quels sont les tarifs? kel son lay ta·reef

(30c) per (30) seconds.
(Trente cents) pour (30) secondes. (tront sent) poor (tront) sgond

I'd like a/an ...	*Je voudrais ...*	zher voo·dray ...
adaptor plug	*une prise*	ewn preez
	multiple	mewl·tee·pler
charger for	*un chargeur pour*	un shar·zher poor
my phone	*mon portable*	mom por·ta·bler
mobile/cell phone	*louer un*	loo·ay um
for hire	*portable*	por·ta·bler
prepaid mobile/	*un portable*	um por·ta·bler
cell phone	*pré-payé*	pray·pay·yay
SIM card for	*une carte SIM*	ewn kart seem
the network	*pour le réseau*	poor ler ray·zo

Internet

Where's the local Internet café?
Où est le cybercafé   oo ay ler see·bair·ka·fay
du coin?   dew kwun

How much per hour?
C'est combien l'heure?   say kom·byun ler

How much per page?
C'est combien la page?   say kom·byun la pazh

Can I burn a CD?
Je peux brûler un CD?   zher per brew·lay un say day

Can you help me change to English-language preference?
Pouvez-vous m'aider à   poo·vay·voo may·day a
choisir l'Anglais comme   shwa·zeer long·glay kom
langue de préférence?   longk der pray·fay·rons

It's crashed.
C'est tombé en panne.   say tom·bay om pan

I'd like to ...	*Je voudrais ...*	zher voo·dray ...
check my email	*consulter mon courrier électronique*	kon·sewl·tay mong koor·yay ay·lek·tro·neek
get Internet access	*me connecter à l'internet*	mer ko·nek·tay a lun·tair·net
use a printer	*utiliser une imprimante*	ew·tee·lee·zay ewn um·pree·mont
use a scanner	*utiliser un scanner*	ew·tee·lee·zay un ska·nair

Do you have ...?	*Avez-vous ...?*	a·vay·voo ...
PCs	*des PCs*	day pay ·say
Macs	*des Macs*	day mak
a zip drive	*une lecteur zip*	ewn lek·ter zeep

GO
Directions

Where's (the station)?
Où est (la gare)?   oo ay (la gar)

Where's (a grocery store)?
Où est-ce qu'il y a (une épicerie)?   oo e· skeel·ya (ewn ay·pee·sree)

I'm looking for the (Metropole Hotel).
Je cherche (L'Hôtel Métropole).   zher shairsh (lo·tel may·tro·pol)

Can you show me (on the map)?
Pouvez-vous m'indiquer   poo·vay·voo mun·dee·kay
(sur la carte)?   (sewr la kart)

What's the address?
Quelle est l'adresse?   kel ay la·dres

How do I get there?
Comment faire pour y aller?   ko·mon fair poor ee a·lay

How far is it?   *C'est loin?*   say lwun

It's ...   *C'est ...*   say ...
  behind ...   *derrière ...*   dair·yair ...
  beside ...   *à côté de ...*   a ko·tay der ...
  far away   *loin d'ici*   lwun dee·see
  here   *ici*   ee·see
  in front of ... *devant ...*   der·von ...
  left   *à gauche*   a gosh
  near here   *près d'ici*   pray dee·see
  on the corner   *au coin*   o kwun
  opposite ...   *en face de ...*   on fas der ...
  right   *à droite*   a drwat
  straight ahead   *tout droit*   too drwa
  there   *là*   la

It's ...	C'est à ...	say ta ...
(10) minutes	(dix) minutes	(dee) mee·newt
(100) metres	(cent) mètres	(son) me·trer

Turn ...	Tournez ...	toor·nay ...
at the corner	au coin	o kwun
at the traffic lights	aux feux	o fer
left	à gauche	a gosh
right	à droite	a drwat

by boat	en bateau	om ba·to
by bus	en bus	om bews
on foot	à pied	a pyay
by metro	en métro	on may·tro
by taxi	en taxi	on tak·see
by train	en train	on trun

north	nord	nor
south	sud	sewd
east	est	est
west	ouest	west

Getting around

What time does the ... leave?	À quelle heure part ...?	a kel er par ...
boat	le bateau	ler ba·to
bus	le bus	ler bews
ferry	le bac	ler bak
plane	l'avion	la·vyon
train	le train	ler trun
tram	le tramway	ler tram·way

What time's the ... bus?	Le ... bus passe à quelle heure?	ler ... bews pas a kel er
first	premier	prer·myay
last	dernier	dair·nyay
next	prochain	pro·shun

How many stops to ...?
Combien d'arrêts jusqu'à ...?   kom·byun da·ray zhews·ka ...

Is this seat taken?
Est-ce que cette place   es·ker set plas
est occupée?   ay o·kew·pay

That's my seat.
C'est ma place.   say ma plas

Can you tell me when we get to ...?
Pouvez-vous me dire quand   poo·vay·voo mer deer kon
nous arrivons à ...?   noo za·ree·von a ...

I want to get off ...	Je veux descendre ...	zher ver day·son·drer ...
at (Nantes)	à (Nantes)	a (nont)
here	ici	ee·see

Tickets & luggage

Where can I buy a ticket?
Où peut-on acheter un billet?   oo per·ton ash·tay um bee·yay

Do I need to book?
Est-ce qu'il faut   es·keel fo
réserver une place?   ray·zer·vay ewn plas

How long does the trip take?
Le trajet dure   ler tra·zhay dewr
combien de temps?   kom·byun der tom

How much is it?	C'est combien?	say kom·byun
I'd like to ... my ticket, please.	Je voudrais ... mon billet, s'il vous plaît.	zher voo·dray ... mom bee·yay seel voo play
cancel	annuler	a·new·lay
change	changer	shon·zhay
collect	passer prendre	pa·say pron·drer
confirm	confirmer	kon·feer·may

One ... ticket (to Lyon), please.	Un billet ... (pour Lyon), s'il vous plaît.	um bee·yay ... (poor lyon) seel voo play
1st-class	de première classe	der prem·yair klas
2nd-class	de seconde classe	der sgond klas
child's	au tarif enfant	o ta·reef on·fon
one-way	simple	sum·pler
return	aller et retour	a·lay ay rer·toor
student's	au tarif étudiant	o ta·reef ay·tew·dyon

I'd like a/an ... seat.	Je voudrais une place ...	zher voo·dray ewn plas ...
aisle	côté couloir	ko·tay koo·lwar
nonsmoking	non-fumeur	non·few·mer
smoking	fumeur	few·mer
window	côté fenêtre	ko·tay fe·ne·trer

GO

Is there air-conditioning?
Est-qu'il y a la climatisation? — es·keel ya la klee·ma·tee·za·syon

Is there a toilet?
Est-qu'il y a des toilettes? — es·keel ya day twa·let

Is it a direct route?
Est-ce que c'est direct? — es·ker say dee·rekt

What time do I have to check in?
Il faut se présenter à
l'enregistrement à quelle heure?
eel fo ser pray·zon·tay a
lon·rer·zhee·strer·mon a kel er

Can I get a stand-by ticket?
Pourrais-je avoir un
ticket stand-by?
poo·rayzh av·war un
tee·ke stond·bai

Where's the baggage claim?
Où est la livraison
des bagages?
oo ay la lee·vray·zon
day ba·gazh

I'd like a luggage locker.
Je voudrais une
consigne automatique.
zher voo·dray ewn
kon·see·nyer o·to·ma·teek

Can I have some coins/tokens?
Je peux avoir des
pièces/jetons?
zher per a·vwar day
pyes/zher·ton

My luggage	*Mes bagages*	may ba·gazh
has been ...	*ont été ...*	on tay·tay ...
damaged	*endommagés*	on·do·ma·zhay
lost	*perdus*	per·dew
stolen	*volés*	vo·lay

Bus, metro, taxi & train

Which bus goes to ...?
Quel bus va à ...?
kel bews va a ...

Is this the bus to ...?
Est-ce que c'est le bus pour ...?
es·ker say ler bews poor ...

What station is this?
C'est quelle gare?
say kel gar

What's the next station?
Quelle est la prochaine gare?   kel ay la pro·shen gar

Does this train stop at (Amboise)?
Est-ce que ce train   es·ker se trun
s'arrête à (Amboise)?   sa·ret a (om·bwaz)

Do I need to change trains?
Est-ce qu'il faut changer de train?   es·keel fo shon·zhay der trun

Which carriage is for (Bordeaux)?
C'est quelle voiture pour   say kel vwa·tewr poor
(Bordeaux)?   (bor·do)

Which line goes to …?
Quelle ligne va à …?   kel lee·nyer va a …

Which platform does it depart from?
Il part de quel quai?   eel par der kel kay

Which is the dining car?
Où est le wagon-restaurant?   oo ay ler va·gon·res·to·ron

Where's the taxi stand?
Où est la station de taxis?   oo ay la sta·syon der tak·see

I'd like a taxi …   *Je voudrais un*   zher voo·dray un
     taxi …   tak·see …
  at (9 o'clock)   *à (neuf heures)*   a (nerf er)
  now   *maintenant*   mun·ter·non
  tomorrow   *demain*   der·mun

Is this taxi free?
Vous êtes libre?   voo zet lee·brer

Please put the meter on.
Mettez le compteur,   me·tay ler kon·ter
s'il vous plaît.   seel voo play

How much is it to …?
C'est combien pour aller à …?   say kom·byun poor a·lay a …

GO

Please take me to (this address).
Conduisez-moi à   kon·dwee·zay mwa a
(cette adresse), s'il vous plaît.   (set a·dres) seel voo play

Please ...	*..., s'il vous plaît.*	... seel voo play
slow down	*Roulez plus*	roo·lay plew
	lentement	lont·mon
wait here	*Attendez ici*	a·ton·day ee·see

Stop ...	*Arrêtez-vous ...*	a·ray·tay voo ...
at the corner	*au coin de la rue*	o kwun der la rew
here	*ici*	ee·see

Car & motorbike hire

I'd like to hire a ...	*Je voudrais louer ...*	zher voo·dray loo·way ...
(small/large) car	*une (petite/ grosse) voiture*	ewn (per·teet/ gros) vwa·tewr
manual	*une manuel*	ewn ma·nwel
motorbike	*une moto*	ewn mo·to

with ...	*avec ...*	a·vek ...
air-conditioning	*climatisation*	klee·ma·tee·za·syon
anti-freeze	*antigel*	on·tee·zhel
snow chains	*chaînes à neige*	shen a nezh

How much for ... hire?	*Quel est le tarif par ...?*	kel ay ler ta·reef par ...
daily	*jour*	zhoor
hourly	*heure*	er
weekly	*semaine*	ser·men

Does that include ...?	*Est-ce que ... est compris(e)?* m/f	es·ker ... ay kom·pree(z)
insurance	*l'assurance* f	la·sew·rons
mileage	*le kilométrage* m	ler kee·lo·may·trazh

What's the speed limit?
Quelle est la vitesse maximale permise?
kel ay la vee·tes mak·see·mal per·meez

Is this the road to ...?
C'est la route pour ...?
say la root poor ...

Where's a petrol station?
Où est-ce qu'il y a une station-service?
oo es·keel ya ewn sta·syon·ser·vees

(How long) Can I park here?
(Combien de temps) Est-ce que je peux stationner ici?
(kom·byun der tom) es·ker zher per sta·syo·nay ee·see

diesel	*diesel* m	dyay·zel
leaded	*au plomb*	o plom
petrol/gas	*essence* f	e·sons
regular	*ordinaire*	or·dee·nair
unleaded	*sans plomb*	son plom

Road signs

Cédez la Priorité	say·day la pree·o·ree·tay	Give Way
Entrée	on·tray	Entrance
Péage	pay·azh	Toll
Sens Interdit	sons un·ter·dee	No Entry
Sens Unique	sons ew·neek	One way
Sortie	sor·tee	Exit
Stop	stop	Stop

SLEEP
Finding accommodation

Where's a ...?	Où est-ce qu'on peut trouver ...?	oo es·kon per troo·vay ...
bed and breakfast	une pension	ewn pon·syon
camping ground	un terrain de camping	un tay·run der kom·peeng
guesthouse	une pension	ewn pon·see·on
hotel	un hôtel	un o·tel
room in a private home	une chambre chez un particulier	ewn shom·brer shay zun par·tee·kew·lyay
youth hostel	une auberge de jeunesse	ewn o·bairzh der zher·nes

Can you recommend somewhere ...?	Est-ce que vous pouvez recommander un logement ...?	es·ker voo poo·vay rer·ko·mon·day un lozh·mon ...
cheap	pas cher	pa shair
nice	agréable	a·gray·a·bler
luxurious	luxueux	lewk·sew·er
nearby	près d'ici	pray dee·see
romantic	romantique	ro·mon·teek

What's the address?
Quelle est l'adresse?   kel ay la·dres

For responses see **GO**, page 46.

Booking ahead & checking in

I'd like to book a room, please.
Je voudrais réserver
une chambre, s'il vous plaît.
zher voo·dray ray·zair·vay
ewn shom·brer seel voo play

I have a reservation.
J'ai une réservation.
zhay ewn ray·zair·va·syon

My name is ...
Mon nom est ...
mon nom ay ...

Do you have	*Avez-vous*	a·vay·voo
a ... room?	*une chambre ...?*	ewn shom·brer ...
double	*avec un grand lit*	a·vek ung gron lee
single	*à un lit*	a un lee
twin	*avec des lits*	a·vek day lee
	jumeaux	zhew·mo

How much	*Quel est*	kel ay
is it per ...?	*le prix par ...?*	ler pree par ...
night	*nuit*	nwee
person	*personne*	per·son
week	*semaine*	ser·men

I'd like to stay for (two) nights.
Je voudrais rester
pour (deux) nuits.
zher voo·dray res·tay
poor (der) nwee

From (July 2) to (July 6).
Du (deux juillet)
au (six juillet).
dew (der zhwee·yay)
o (see zhwee·yay)

There are (three) of us.
Nous sommes (trois).
noo som (trwa)

Can I see it?
Est-ce que je peux la voir?
es·ker zher per la vwar

It's fine, I'll take it.
C'est bien, je la prends. say byun zher la pron

Do I need to pay upfront?
Est-ce qu'il faut payer par avance? es·keel fo pay·yay par a·vons

Can I pay by ...?	*Est-ce qu'on peut payer avec ...?*	es·kom per pay·yay a·vek ...
credit card	*une carte de crédit*	ewn kart der kray·dee
travellers cheque	*des chèques de voyage*	day shek der vwa·yazh

Requests & queries

When/Where is breakfast served?
Quand/Où le petit déjeuner est-il servi? kon/oo ler per·tee day·zher·nay ay·teel sair·vee

Please wake me at (seven).
Réveillez-moi à (sept) heures, s'il vous plaît. ray·vay·yay·mwa a (set) er seel voo play

Could I have my key, please?
Puis-je avoir ma clé, s'il vous plaît. pweezh av·war ma klay seel voo play

Could I have a receipt, please?
Puis-je avoir un reçu, s'il vous plaît? pweezh av·war un v seel voo play

Can I use the ...?	*Est-ce que je peux utiliser ...?*	es·ker zher per ew·tee·lee·zay ...
kitchen	*la cuisine*	la kwee·zeen
laundry	*la blanchisserie*	la blon·shees·ree
telephone	*le téléphone*	ler tay·lay·fon

Do you have a/an ...?	*Avez-vous ...?*	a·vay·voo ...
elevator	*un ascenseur*	un a·son·ser
safe	*un coffre-fort*	ung ko·frer·for

Do you change money here?
Échangez-vous l'argent ici?   ay·shon·zhay·voo lar·zhon ee·see

Do you arrange tours here?
Organisez-vous des excursions ici?   or·ga·nee·zay·voo day zeks·kewr·syon ee·see

It's too ...	*C'est trop ...*	say tro ...
cold	*froid*	frwa
dark	*sombre*	som·brer
expensive	*cher*	shair
light/bright	*clair*	klair
noisy	*bruyant*	brew·yon
small	*petit*	per·tee

Can I get another ...?	*Est-ce que je peux avoir un/une autre ...?* m/f	es·ker zher per a·vwar un/ewn o·trer ...
This ... isn't clean.	*Ce/Cette ... n'est pas propre.* m/f	ser/set ... nay pa pro·prer
blanket	*couverture* f	koo·vair·tewr
pillow	*oreiller* m	o·ray·yay
pillowcase	*taie* f *d'oreiller*	tay do·ray·yay
sheet	*drap* m	drap
towel	*serviette* f	sair·vee·et

The ... doesn't work.	*... ne fonctionne pas.*	... ner fong·syon pa
air-conditioning	*La climatisation*	la klee·ma·tee·za·syon
fan	*Le ventilateur*	ler von·tee·la·ter
toilet	*Les toilettes*	lay twa·let
window	*La fenêtre*	la fer·ne·trer

Checking out

What time is checkout?
Quand faut-il régler?   kon fo·teel ray·glay

Can I have a late checkout?
Pourrai-je régler plus tard?   poo·rezh ray·glay plew tar

Can I leave my luggage here until ...?	Puis-je laisser mes bagages jusqu'à ...?	pweezh lay·say may ba·gazh zhews·ka ...
next week	la semaine prochaine	la ser·men pro·shen
tonight	ce soir	ser swar
Wednesday	mercredi	mair·krer·dee

Could I have my ..., please?	Est-ce que je pourrais avoir ..., s'il vous plaît?	es·ker zher poo·ray a·vwar ... seel voo play
deposit	ma caution	ma ko·syon
passport	mon passeport	mon pas·por
valuables	mes biens précieux	may byun pray·syer

I'll be back ...	Je retournerai ...	zher rer·toor·ner·ray ...
in (three) days	dans (trois) jours	don (trwa) zhur
on (Tuesday)	(mardi)	(mar·dee)

I had a great stay, thank you.
J'ai fait un séjour magnifique, merci.   zhay fay un say·zhoor ma·nyee·feek mair·see

I'll recommend it to my friends.
Je le recommanderai à mes amis.   zher ler rer·ko·mon·dray a may za·mee

WORK
Introductions

I'm attending a ...	Je participe à un/une ... m/f	zhe par·tee·seep a un/ewn ...
Where's the ...?	Où est le/la ...? m/f	oo ay ler/la ...
business centre	centre m d'affaires	son·trer da·fair
conference	conférence f	kon·fay·rons
course	stage m	stazh
meeting	réunion f	ray·ew·nyon
trade fair	foire f commerciale	fwar ko·mair·syal
I'm with ...	Je suis avec ...	zher swee a·vek ...
(the UN)	(l'ONU)	(lo en oo)
my colleague(s)	mon/ma collègue m/f	mong/ma ko·leg
	mes collègue(s) m&f pl	may ko·leg
(two) others	(deux) autres	(derz) o·trer

Here's my business card.
Voici ma carte.
vwa·see ma kart

Let me introduce my colleague.
Permettez-moi de vous
présenter mon/ma collègue. m/f
pair·may·tay mwa de voo
pray·zon·tay mon/ma ko·leg

I'm alone
Je suis seul(e). m/f
zher swee serl

I'm staying at ..., room ...
Je loge à ..., chambre ...
zher lozh a ... shom·brer ...

I'm here for (two) days/weeks.
Je suis ici pour
(deux) jours/semaines.
zher swee·zee·see poor
(der) zhoor/ser·men

Business needs

I have an appointment with …
J'ai rendez-vous avec …　　zhay ron·day·voo a·vek …

I'm expecting a fax/call.
Je attends un fax/appel.　　zha·ton un faks/a·pel

I need an interpreter.
J'ai besoin d'un interprète.　　zhay ber·zwun dun un·tair·pret

I'd like …	*Je voudrais …*	zher voo·dray …
a connection	*me connecter à*	mer ko·nek·tay a
to the internet	*l'internet*	lun·tair·net
to use a computer	*utiliser un*	ew·tee·lee·zay un
	ordinateur	or·dee·na·ter
to send an	*envoyer un*	en·vwa·yay un
email/fax	*email/fax*	e·mayl/faks

Is there a/an …?	*Y a-t-il …?*	ya·teel …
data projector	*un projecteur data*	um pro·zhek·ter da·ta
laser pointer	*un pointeur laser*	un pwun·ter la·zair
overhead projector	*un rétroprojecteur*	un ray·tro·pro·zhek·ter
whiteboard	*un tableau blanc*	un ta·blo blon

After the deal

That went very well.
Ça s'est très bien passé.　　sa say tray byun pa·say

Shall we go for a drink?
On prend un verre?　　om pron tun vair

Shall we go for a meal?
On va manger?　　on va mon·zhay

It's on me.
C'est moi qui offre.　　say mwa kee o·frer

HELP
Emergencies

Help!	*Au secours!*	o skoor
Stop!	*Arrêtez!*	a·ray·tay
Go away!	*Allez-vous-en!*	a·lay·voo·zon
Thief!	*Au voleur!*	o vo·ler
Fire!	*Au feu!*	o fer
Watch out!	*Faites attention!*	fet a·ton·syon

Call ...	*Appelez ...*	a·play ...
an ambulance	*une ambulance*	ewn omb·ew·lons
a doctor	*un médecin*	un mayd·sun
the fire brigade	*les pompiers*	lay pom·pyay
the police	*la police*	la po·lees

It's an emergency!
C'est urgent!   say tewr·zhon

Could you help me, please?
Est-ce que vous pourriez   es·ker voo poo·ryay
m'aider, s'il vous plaît?   may·day seel voo play

Could I use the telephone?
Est-ce que je pourrais   es·ker zher poo·ray
utiliser le téléphone?   ew·tee·lee·zay ler tay·lay·fon

I'm lost.
Je suis perdu(e). m/f   zher swee pair·dew

Where are the toilets?
Où sont les toilettes?   oo son lay twa·let

Leave me alone!
Laissez-moi tranquille!   lay·say·mwa trong·keel

Police

Where's the police station?
Où est le commissariat de police?
oo ay ler ko·mee·sar·ya der po·lees

I want to report an offence.
Je veux signaler un délit.
zher ver see·nya·lay un day·lee

I've been raped.
J'ai été violé(e). m/f
zhay ay·tay vyo·lay

I've been assaulted.
J'ai été violenté(e). m/f
zhay ay·tay vyo·lon·tay

I've been robbed.
On m'a volé.
on ma vo·lay

I want to contact my embassy/consulate.
Je veux contacter mon ambassade/consulat.
zher ver kon·tak·tay mon om·ba·sad/kon·sew·la

I've lost my ...	*J'ai perdu ...*	zhay pair·dew ...
My ... was/were stolen.	*On m'a volé ...*	on ma vo·lay ...
backpack	*mon sac à dos*	mon sak a do
bags	*mes valises*	may va·leez
credit card	*ma carte de crédit*	ma kart der kray·dee
handbag	*mon sac à main*	mon sak a mun
jewellery	*mes bijoux*	may bee·zhoo
money	*mon argent*	mon ar·zhon
passport	*mon passeport*	mom pas·por
travellers cheques	*mes chèques de voyage*	may shek der vwa·yazh
wallet	*mon portefeuille*	mom por·ter·fer·yer

I have insurance.
Je suis assuré(e). m/f   zher sweez a·sew·ray

Can I have a receipt for my insurance?
Puis-je avoir le reçu   pweezh a·vwar ler rer·sew
pour mon assurance?   poor mon a·sew·rons

I have a prescription for this drug.
On m'a prescrit cette drogue.   om ma pray·skree set drog

Health

Where's a	*Où y a t-il*	oo ee a teel
nearby …?	*un/une … par ici?* m/f	un/ewn … par ee·see
(night) chemist	*pharmacie* f	far·ma·see
	(de nuit)	(der nwee)
dentist	*dentiste* m&f	don·teest
doctor	*médecin* m&f	mayd·sun
hospital	*hôpital* m	o·pee·tal
medical centre	*centre* m	son·trer
	médical	may·dee·kal
optometrist	*optométriste* m&f	op·to·may·treest

I need a doctor (who speaks English).
J'ai besoin d'un médecin   zhay ber·zwun dun mayd·sun
(qui parle anglais).   (kee parl ong·glay)

Could I see a female doctor?
Est-ce que je peux voir   es·ker zher per vwar
une femme médecin?   ewn fam mayd·sun

Can the doctor come here?
Est-ce que le médecin   es·ker ler mayd·sun
peut venir ici?   per ver·neer ee·see

I've run out of my medication.
Je n'ai plus de — zher nay plew der
médicaments. — may·dee·ka·mon

My prescription is ...
Mon ordonnance indique ... — mo nor·do·nons on·deek ...

I've been	*Je me suis fait*	zher mer swee fay
vaccinated	*vacciner*	vak·see·nay
against ...	*contre ...*	kon·trer ...
hepatitis	*l'hépatite*	lay·pa·teet
tetanus	*le tétanos*	ler tay·ta·nos
typhoid	*la typhoïde*	la tee·fo·eed

I need new ...	*J'ai besoin de*	zhay ber·zwun der
	nouvelles ...	noo·vel ...
contact lenses	*lentilles*	lon·tee·yer
	de contact	der kon·takt
glasses	*lunettes*	lew·net

Symptoms, conditions & allergies

I'm sick.
Je suis malade. — zher swee ma·lad

I've been injured.
J'ai été blessé(e). m/f — zhay ay·tay blay·say

It hurts here.
J'ai une douleur ici. — zhay ewn doo·ler ee·see

I've been vomiting.
J'ai vomi. — zhay vo·mee

I can't sleep.
Je n'arrive pas à dormir. zher na·reev pa a dor·meer

I feel ...   *Je me sens ...*   zher mer son ...
  anxious   *inquiet/*   un·kyay/
   inquiète m/f   un·kyet
  better   *mieux*   myer
  weak   *faible*   fe·bler
  worse   *plus mal*   plew mal

I feel ...   *J'ai ...*   zhay ...
  dizzy   *des vertiges*   day ver·teezh
  hot and cold   *chaud et froid*   sho ay frwa
  nauseous   *des nausées*   day no·zay
  shivery   *des frissons*   day free·son

I have (a/an) ...   *J'ai ...*   zhay ...
  allergy   *une allergie*   ewn a·lair·zhee
  asthma   *de l'asthme*   de las·mer
  bronchitis   *une bronchite*   ewn bron·sheet
  cold   *un rhume*   un rewm
  cough   *une toux*   ewn too
  diabetes   *du diabète*   dew dya·bet
  diarrhoea   *la diarrhée*   la dya·ray
  fever   *de la fièvre*   der la fyay·vrer
  headache   *mal à la tête*   mal a la tet
  heart condition   *une condition*   ewn kon·dee·syon
   cardiaque   kar·dyak
  sore throat   *mal à la gorge*   mal a la gorzh
  swelling   *un gonflement*   un gon·fler·mon
  venereal   *une maladie*   ewn ma·la·dee
   disease   *vénérienne*   vay·nay·ryen

I've recently had ...
J'ai eu récemment ...   zher ew ray·sa·mon ...

I'm on medication for ...
Je prends des   zher pron day
médicaments pour ...   may·dee·ka·mon poor ...

I need something for ...
J'ai besoin d'un   zhay ber·zwun dun
médicament pour ...   may·dee·ka·mom poor ...

Do I need a prescription for ...?
J'ai besoin d'une   zhay ber·zwun dewn
ordonnance pour ...?   or·do·nons poor ...

How many times a day?
Combien de fois par jour?   kom·byun der fwa par zhoor

I'm allergic to ...   *Je suis*   zher swee
                          allergique ...   za·lair·zheek ...

antibiotics	*aux antibiotiques*	o zon·tee·byo·teek
anti-	*aux anti-*	o zun·tee·
inflammatories	*inflammatoires*	un·fla·ma·twar
aspirin	*à l'aspirine*	a las·pee·reen
bees	*aux abeilles*	o za·bay·yer
codeine	*à la codéine*	a la ko·day·een
penicillin	*à la pénicilline*	a la payn·nee·see·leen
pollen	*au pollen*	o po·len

I have a skin allergy.
J'ai une allergie de peau.   zhay ewn a·lair·zhee der po

For food-related allergies, see **EAT & DRINK**, page 32.

HELP

66

Numbers

0	*zéro*	zay·ro		18	*dix-huit*	dee·zweet
1	*un*	un		19	*dix-neuf*	deez·nerf
2	*deux*	der		20	*vingt*	vung
3	*trois*	trwa		21	*vingt et un*	vung tay un
4	*quatre*	ka·trer		22	*vingt-deux*	vung·der
5	*cinq*	sungk		30	*trente*	tront
6	*six*	sees		40	*quarante*	ka·ront
7	*sept*	set		50	*cinquante*	sung·kont
8	*huit*	weet		60	*soixante*	swa·sont
9	*neuf*	nerf		70	*soixante-dix*	swa·son·dees
10	*dix*	dees		71	*soixante-et-onze*	swa·sont·et·onz
11	*onze*	onz		80	*quatre-vingts*	ka·trer·vung
12	*douze*	dooz		90	*quatre-vingt-*	ka·trer·vung·
13	*treize*	trez			*dix*	dees
14	*quatorze*	ka·torz				
15	*quinze*	kunz		100	*cent*	son
16	*seize*	sez		1,000	*mille*	meel
17	*dix-sept*	dee·set		1,000,000	*un million*	um meel·yon

Colours

black	*noir(e)*	nwar		**pink**	*rose*	roz
blue	*bleu(e)*	bler		**purple**	*violet/*	vyo·lay/
brown	*brun/*	brun/			*violette*	vyo·let
	brune	brewn		**red**	*rouge*	roozh
green	*vert(e)*	vair(t)		**white**	*blanc(he)*	blon(sh)
orange	*orange*	o·ronzh		**yellow**	*jaune*	zhon

67

Time & dates

What time is it?	Quelle heure est-il?	kel er ay·teel
It's (one) o'clock.	Il est (une) heure.	ee·lay (ewn) er
It's (10) o'clock.	Il est (dix) heures.	ee·lay (deez) er
Quarter past one.	Il est une heure et quart.	ee·lay ewn eray kar
Twenty past one.	Il est une heure vingt.	ee·lay ewn er vung
Half past one.	Il est une heure et demie.	ee·lay ewn er ay der·mee
Twenty to one.	Il est une heure moins vingt.	ee·lay ewn er mwun vung
Quarter to one.	Il est une heure moins le quart	ee·lay ewn er mwun ler kar
At what time?	À quelle heure?	a kel er

Monday	lundi	lun·dee
Tuesday	mardi	mar·dee
Wednesday	mercredi	mair·krer·dee
Thursday	jeudi	zher·dee
Friday	vendredi	von·drer·dee
Saturday	samedi	sam·dee
Sunday	dimanche	dee·monsh

January	janvier	zhon·vyay
February	février	fayv·ryay
March	mars	mars
April	avril	a·vreel
May	mai	may
June	juin	zhwun
July	juillet	zhwee·yay
August	août	oot
September	septembre	sep·tom·brer
October	octobre	ok·to·brer
November	novembre	no·vom·brer
December	décembre	day·som·brer

spring	*printemps* m	prun·tom
summer	*été* m	ay·tay
autumn	*automne* m	o·ton
winter	*hiver* m	ee·vair

What date?
Quelle date?　　　　　　　　　kel dat

What's today's date?
C'est quel jour aujourd'hui?　　say kel zhoor o·zhoor·dwee

It's (18 October).
C'est le (dix-huit octobre).　　say ler (dee·zwee tok·to·brer)

last ...		
month	*le mois dernier*	ler mwa dair·nyay
night	*hier soir*	ee·yair swar
week	*la semaine dernière*	la ser·men dair·nyair
year	*l'année dernière*	la·nay dair·nyair

next ...		
month	*le mois prochain*	ler mwa pro·shen
week	*la semaine prochaine*	la se·men pro·shen
year	*l'année prochaine*	la·nay pro·shen

| since (May) | *depuis (mai)* | der·pwee (may) |

tomorrow ...	*demain ...*	der·mun ...
afternoon	*après-midi*	a·pray·mee·dee
evening	*soir*	swar
morning	*matin*	ma·tun

yesterday ...	*hier ...*	ee·yair ...
afternoon	*après-midi*	a·pray·mee·dee
evening	*soir*	swar
morning	*matin*	ma·tun

Nouns in this dictionary have their gender indicated by m (masculine) or f (feminine).
If it's a plural noun, you'll also see pl.
Where no gender is marked the word is either an adjective or a verb, with adjectives first.

A

aboard *à bord* a bor
accident *accident* m ak·see·don
accommodation *logement* m lozh·mon
account *compte* m kont
adaptor *adaptateur* m a·dap·ta·ter
address *adresse* f a·dres
admission (price) *prix* m *d'entrée* pree
   don·tray
after *après* a·pray
afternoon *après-midi* ma·pray·mee·dee
aftershave *après-rasage* m a·pray·ra·zazh
again *encore* ong·kor
air-conditioned *climatisé(e)* m/f
   klee·ma·tee·zay
airline *ligne* f *aérienne* lee·nyer a·ay·ryen
airmail *par avion* par a·vyon
airplane *avion* m a·vyon
airport *aéroport* m a·ay·ro·por
aisle (on plane, etc) *couloir* m koo·lwar
alarm clock *réveil* m ray·vay
alcohol *alcool* m al·kol
all *tout(e)* m/f too(t)
allergy *allergie* f a·lair·zhee
almonds *amandes* f pl a·mond
alone *tout(e) seul(e)* m/f too(t) serl
ambulance *ambulance* f om·bew·lons
American *américain/américaine* m/f
   a·may·ree·kun/a·may·ree·ken
and *et* ay
ankle *cheville* f sher·vee·yer
another *un/une autre* m/f un/ewn o·trer
antibiotics *antibiotiques* m pl
   on·tee·byo·teek
antiseptic *antiseptique* m on·tee·sep·teek
apartment *appartement* m a·par·ter·mon
apple *pomme* f pom
appointment *rendez-vous* m ron·day·voo
apricot *abricot* m a·bree·ko

architect *architecte* m&f ar·shee·tekt
architecture *architecture* f
   ar·shee·tek·tewr
arm *bras* m bra
arrivals *arrivées* f pl a·ree·vay
art *art* m ar
art gallery *musée* m • *galerie* f mew·zay
   • gal·ree
artist *artiste* m&f ar·teest
ashtray *cendrier* m son·dree·yay
aspirin *aspirine* f as·pee·reen
at *à* a
aunt *tante* f tont
Australia *Australie* f o·stra·lee
autumn *automne* m o·ton
automatic teller machine (ATM) *guichet*
   m *automatique de banque (GAB)* gee·shay
   o·to·ma·teek der bonk

B

B&W (film) *noir et blanc* nwar ay blong
baby *bébé* m bay·bay
baby food *bouillie* f boo·yee
babysitter *baby-sitter* m&f ba·bee·see·ter
back (body) *dos* m do
backpack *sac* m *à dos* sak a do
bacon *lard* m lar
bad *mauvais(e)* m/f mo·vay(z)
bag *sac* m sak
baggage *bagages* m pl ba·gazh
baggage allowance *franchise* f
   fron·sheez
baggage claim *retrait* m *des bagages*
   rer·tray day ba·gazh
bakery *boulangerie* f boo·lon·zhree
banana *banane* f ba·nan
band (music) *bande* f bond
bandage *pansement* m pons·mon

Band-Aid *sparadrap* m spa·ra·dra
bank *banque* f bonk
bank account *compte* m *bancaire* kont bong·kair
banknote *billet* m *de banque* bee·yay der bonk
bar *bar* m bar
bath *baignoire* f be·nywar
bathroom *salle* f *de bain* sal der bun
battery *pile* f peel
beach *plage* f plazh
beans (French) *haricots* m pl *verts* a·ree·ko ver
beautiful *beau/belle* m/f bo/bel
beauty salon *salon* m *de beauté* sa·lon der bo·tay
bed *lit* m lee
bed linen *draps* m pl dra
bedroom *chambre* f *à coucher* shom·brer a koo·shay
beef *bœuf* m berf
beer *bière* f byair
before *avant* a·von
behind *derrière* dair·yair
beside *à côté de* a ko·tay der
best *le/la meilleur(e)* m/f ler/la may·yer
better *meilleur(e)* m/f may·yer
bicycle *vélo* m vay·lo
big *grand(e)* m/f gron(d)
bigger *plus grand(e)* m/f plew gron(d)
biggest *le/la plus grand(e)* m/f ler/la plew gron(d)
bill (restaurant) *addition* f a·dee·syon
birthday *anniversaire* m a·nee·vair·sair
bitter *amer/amère* m/f a·mair
blanket *couverture* f koo·vair·tewr
blister *ampoule* f om·pool
blocked *bloqué(e)* m/f blo·kay
blood *sang* m son
blood group *groupe* m *sanguin* groop song·gun
board (a plane, ship) *monter à bord* mon·tay a bor

boarding house *pension* f pon·syon
boarding pass *carte* f *d'embarquement* kart dom·bar·ker·mon
boat *bateau* m ba·to
book *livre* m leev·rer
book (make a booking) *réserver* ray·zair·vay
booked up *complet/complète* m/f kom·play/kom·plet
bookshop *librairie* f lee·bray·ree
boots *bottes* f pl bot
border *frontière* f fron·tyair
boring *ennuyeux/ennuyeuse* m/f on·nwee·yer/on·nwee·yerz
both *tous les deux* too lay der
bottle *bouteille* f boo·tay
bottle opener *ouvre-bouteille* m oo·vrer·boo·tay
bowl *bol* m bol
box *boîte* f bwat
boy *garçon* m gar·son
boyfriend *petit ami* m per·tee a·mee
bra *soutien-gorge* m soo·tyung·gorzh
brakes *freins* m frun
bread *pain* m pun
breakfast *petit déjeuner* m per·tee day·zher·nay
bridge *pont* m pon
briefcase *serviette* f sair·vyet
brochure *brochure* f bro·shewr
broken *cassé(e)* m/f ka·say
broken down *(tombé) en panne* (tom·bay) on pan
brother *frère* m frair
brown *brun/brune* m/f brun/brewn
brush *brosse* f bros
budget *budget* m bew·dzay
buffet *buffet* m bew·fay
building *bâtiment* m ba·tee·mon
burn *brûlure* f brew·lewr
bus (city) *(auto)bus* m (o·to)bews
bus (intercity) *(auto)car* m (o·to)kar
bus station *gare* f *routière* gar roo·tyair
bus stop *arrêt* m *d'autobus* a·ray do·to·bews

C English–French dictionary

business *affaires* f pl a·fair
business class *classe f affaires* klas a·fair
business man/woman *homme/femme m/f d'affaires* om/fam da·fair
business trip *voyage m d'affaires* vwa·yazh da·fair
busy *occupé(e)* m/f o·kew·pay
butcher's shop *boucherie* f boosh·ree
butter *beurre* m ber
button *bouton* m boo·ton
buy *acheter* ash·tay

C

cabbage *chou* m shoo
café *café* m ka·fay
cake shop *pâtisserie* f pa·tees·ree
calculator *calculatrice* f kal·kew·la·trees
call *appeler* a·pe·lay
camera *appareil m photo* a·pa·ray fo·to
camping ground *camping* m kom·peeng
camp site *terrain m de camping* tay·run der kom·peeng
can (tin) *boîte* f bwat
can opener *ouvre-boîte* m oo·vrer·bwat
Canada *Canada* m ka·na·da
cancel *annuler* a·new·lay
capsicum *poivron* m pwa·vron
car *voiture* f vwa·tewr
car hire *location f de voitures* lo·ka·syon der vwa·tewr
car owner's title *carte f grise* kart greez
car registration *immatriculation* ee·ma·tree·kew·la·syon
carpark *parking* m par·keeng
carrot *carotte* f ka·rot
cash *argent* m ar·zhon
cash (a cheque) *encaisser* ong·kay·say
cash register *caisse f (enregistreuse)* kes (on·rer·zhee·strerz)
cashier *caissier/caissière* m/f ke·syay/ke·syair
cassette *cassette* f ka·set

castle *château* m sha·to
cathedral *cathédrale* f ka·tay·dral
CD *CD* m say·day
centre *centre* m son·trer
cereal *céréales* m pl say·ray·al
chair *chaise* f shez
chairlift (skiing) *télésiège* m tay·lay·syezh
champagne *champagne* m shom·pa·nyer
change (coins) *monnaie* f mo·nay
change (money) *échanger* ay·shon·zhay
change (general) *changer* shon·zhay
changing room *cabine f d'essayage* ka·been day·say·yazh
cheap *bon marché* m bon mar·shay
check (banking) *chèque* m shek
check (bill) *addition* f a·dee·syon
check-in (desk) *enregistrement* on·rer·zhee·strer·mon
cheese *fromage* m fro·mazh
chef *chef m de cuisine* shef der kwee·zeen
chemist (place) *pharmacie* f far·ma·see
chemist (person) *pharmacien(ne)* m/f far·ma·syun/far·ma·syen
cheque (banking) *chèque* m shek
cherry *cerises* f se·rees
chest *poitrine* f pwa·treen
chicken *poulet* m poo·lay
child *enfant* m/f on·fon
child seat *siège m pour enfant* syezh poor on·fon
childminding *garderie* f gard·ree
children *enfants* m/f pl on·fon
chocolate *chocolat* m sho·ko·la
Christmas *Noël* m no·el
church *église* f ay·gleez
cigar *cigare* m see·gar
cigarette *cigarette* f see·ga·ret
cigarette lighter *briquet* m bree·kay
cinema *cinéma* m see·nay·ma
circus *cirque* m seerk
city *ville* f veel
city centre *centre-ville* m son·trer·veel
clean *propre* pro·prer
clean *nettoyer* net·wa·yay

cleaning *nettoyage* m net·wa·yazh
client *client(e)* m/f klee·on(t)
cloakroom *vestiaire* m vays·tyair
close *près* pray
close *fermer* fair·may
closed *fermé(e)* m/f fair·may
clothing *vêtements* m pl vet·mon
clothing store *magasin* m *de vêtements* ma·ga·zun der vet·mon
coat *manteau* m mon·to
cocktail *cocktail* m kok·tel
coffee *café* m ka·fay
coins *pièces* f pl pyes
cold *froid(e)* m/f frwa(d)
colleague *collègue* m/f ko·leg
collect call *appel* m *en PCV* a·pel on pay·say·vay
colour *couleur* f koo·ler
comb *peigne* m pe·nyer
comfortable *confortable* kon·for·ta·bler
companion *compagnon/compagne* m/f kom·pa·nyon/kom·pa·nyer
company *entreprise* f on·trer·preez
complaint *plainte* f plunt
complimentary (free) *gratuit(e)* m/f gra·twee(t)
computer *ordinateur* m or·dee·na·ter
concert *concert* m kon·sair
concussion *commotion* f *cérébrale* ko·mo·syon say·ray·bral
conditioner (hair) *après-shampooing* m a·pray·shom·pwung
condom *préservatif* m pray·zair·va·teef
conference (big) *congrès* m kong·gray
conference (small) *colloque* m ko·lok
confirm (a booking) *confirmer* kon·feer·may
congratulations *félicitations* fay·lee·see·ta·syon
connection *rapport* m ra·por
constipation *constipation* f kon·stee·pa·syon
consulate *consulat* m kon·sew·la
contact lenses *verres de contact* m pl vair der kon·takt

convenience store *supérette* f *de quartier* sew·pay·ret der kar·tyay
cook *cuisinier/cuisinière* m/f kwee·zee·nyay/kwee·zee·nyair
cook *cuire* kweer
cool *frais/fraîche* m/f fray/fresh
corkscrew *tire-bouchon* m teer·boo·shon
cost *coût* m koo
cotton *coton* m ko·ton
cotton balls *ouate* f *de coton* wat der ko·ton
cough *toux* f too
cough medicine *sirop* m *contre la toux* see·ro kon·trer la too
countryside *campagne* f kom·pa·nyer
court (tennis) *court* m koor
cover charge *couvert* m koo·vair
crafts *artisanat* m ar·tee·za·na
cream *crème* f krem
crèche *crèche* f kresh
credit *crédit* m kray·dee
credit card *carte* f *de crédit* kart der kray·dee
cup *tasse* f tas
currency exchange *taux* m *de change* to der shonzh
current (electricity) *courant* m koo·ron
custom *coutume* f koo·tewm
customs *douane* f dwan
cutlery *couverts* m pl koo·vair

D

daily *quotidien(ne)* m/f ko·tee·dyun/ko·tee·dyen
dance f *danse* dons
dance *danser* don·say
dancing *danse* f dons
dangerous *dangereux/dangereuse* m/f don·zhrer/don·zhrerz
dark *obscur(e)* m/f ob·skewr
dark (of colour) *foncé(e)* m/f fon·say
date (day) *date* f dat

date of birth *date* f *de naissance* dat der
   nay·sons
daughter *fille* f fee·yer
dawn *aube* f ob
day *jour* m zhoor
day after tomorrow (the) *après-demain*
   a·pray·der·mun
day before yesterday (the) *avant-hier*
   a·von·tyair
delay *retard* m rer·tard
delicatessen *traiteur* m tre·ter
deliver *livrer* leev·ray
dental floss *fil* m *dentaire* feel don·tair
dentist *dentiste* m&f don·teest
deodorant *déodorant* m day·o·do·ron
depart (leave) *partir* par·teer
department store *grand magasin* m gron
   ma·ga·zun
departure *départ* m day·par
deposit *dépôt* m day·po
destination *destination* f des·tee·na·syon
diabetes *diabète* m dya·bet
dial tone *tonalité* f to·na·lee·tay
diaper *couche* f koosh
diarrhoea *diarrhée* f dya·ray
diary *agenda* m a·zhun·da
dictionary *dictionnaire* m deek·syo·nair
different *différent(e)* m/f dee·fay·ron(t)
dinner *dîner* m dee·nay
direct *direct(e)* m/f dee·rekt
direct-dial *composition* f *directe*
   kom·po·zees·yon dee·rekt
direction *direction* f dee·rek·syon
dirty *sale* sal
disabled *handicapé(e)* m/f on·dee·ka·pay
discount *remise* f rer·meez
dish *plat* m pla
disk (CD-ROM) *disque* m deesk
disk (floppy) *disquette* f dees·ket
doctor *médecin* m&f mayd·sun
dog *chien* m shyun
dollar *dollar* m do·lar
dope (drugs) *drogue* f drog

double bed *grand lit* m gron lee
double room *chambre* f *pour deux personnes*
   shom·brer poor der pair·son
dress *robe* f rob
drink *boisson* f bwa·son
drink *boire* bwar
drink (alcoholic) *verre* m vair
drive *conduire* kon·dweer
drivers licence *permis* m *de conduire*
   pair·mee der kon·dweer
drug *drogue* f drog
drunk *ivre* ee·vrer
dry *sec/sèche* m/f sek/sesh
dry *sécher* say·shay
duck *canard* m
dummy (pacifier) *tétine* f tay·teen

E

each *chaque* shak
ear *oreille* f o·ray
early *tôt* to
earrings *boucles* f pl *d'oreille* boo·kler
   do·ray
east *est* m est
Easter *Pâques* pak
eat *manger* mon·zhay
economy class *classe* f *touriste* klas
   too·reest
egg *œuf* m erf
electrical store *magasin* m *qui vend des
   appareils électriques* ma·ga·zun kee von
   day za·pa·ray ay·lek·treek
electricity *électricité* f ay·lek·tree·see·tay
elevator *ascenseur* m a·son·ser
email *e-mail* m ay·mel
embassy *ambassade* f om·ba·sad
emergency *cas* m *urgent* ka ewr·zhon
empty *vide* veed
end *finir* fee·neer
engaged *fiancé(e)* m/f fyon·say
engagement *fiançailles* f pl fyon·sai
engine *moteur* m mo·ter

LOOK UP

engineer *ingénieur* m un-zhay-nyer
engineering *ingénierie* f un-zhay-nee-ree
England *Angleterre* f ong-gler-tair
English *anglais(e)* m/f ong-glay(z)
enough *assez* a-say
enter *entrer* on-tray
entertainment guide *programme* m *des spectacles* pro-gram day spek-tak-ler
entry *entrée* f on-tray
envelope *enveloppe* f on-vlop
escalator *escalier* m *roulant* es-ka-lyay roo-lon
estate agency *agence* f *immobilière* a-zhons ee-mo-bee-lyair
euro *euro* m er-ro
Europe *Europe* f er-rop
evening *soir* m swar
every *chaque* shak
everyone *tout le monde* too ler mond
everything *tout* too
exactly *exactement* eg-zak-ter-mon
excess (baggage) *excédent* ek-say-don
exchange *échange* m ay-shonzh
exchange *échanger* ay-shon-zhay
exchange rate *taux* m *de change* to der shonzh
exhibition *exposition* f ek-spo-zee-syon
exit *sortie* f sor-tee
expensive *cher/chère* m/f shair
express (mail) *exprès* eks-pres
eye *œil* m er-yee
eyes *yeux* m yer

F

face *visage* m vee-zazh
fall (autumn) *automne* m o-ton
family *famille* f fa-mee-yer
family name *nom* m *de famille* non der fa-mee-yer
fan (machine) *ventilateur* m von-tee-la-ter
far *loin* lwun

fare *tarif* m ta-reef
fashion *mode* f mod
fast *rapide* ra-peed
fat *gras(se)* m/f gra(s)
father *père* m pair
faucet *robinet* m ro-bee-nay
faulty *défectueux/défectueuse* m/f day-fek-twer/day-fek-twerz
fax *fax* m faks
feel (touch) *toucher* too-shay
feeling (physical) *sensation* f son-sa-syon
female *femelle* fer-mel
ferry *bac* m bak
fever *fièvre* f fyev-rer
fiancé *fiancé* m fyon-say
fiancée *fiancée* f fyon-say
film (cinema) *film* m feelm
film (for camera) *pellicule* f pay-lee-kewl
film speed *sensibilité* f *de la pellicule* son-see-bee-lee-tay der la pay-lee-kewl
fine (penalty) *amende* f a-mond
finger *doigt* m dwa
first class *première classe* f prer-myair klas
first-aid kit *trousse* f *à pharmacie* troos a far-ma-see
fish *poisson* m pwa-son
fish shop *poissonnerie* f pwa-son-ree
fishing *pêche* f pesh
flashlight *lampe* f *de poche* lomp der posh
fleamarket *marché* m *aux puces* mar-shay o pews
flight *vol* m vol
floor (storey) *étage* m ay-tazh
florist *fleuriste* m/f fler-reest
flu *grippe* f greep
fly *mouche* f moosh
food *nourriture* f noo-ree-tewr
foot *pied* m pyay
football (soccer) *football* m foot-bol
footpath *sentier* m son-tyay
foreign *étranger/étrangère* m/f ay-tron-zhay/ay-tron-zhair

forest *forêt* f fo·ray
fork *fourchette* f foor·shet
fortnight *quinze jours* m pl kunz zhoor
fragile *fragile* fra·zheel
France *la France* f la frons
free (available) *disponible* dees·po·nee·bler
free (gratis) *gratuit(e)* m/f gra·twee(t)
French *Français(e)* m/f fron·say(z)
fresh *frais/fraîche* m/f fray/fresh
fridge *réfrigérateur* m ray·free·zhay·ra·ter
friend *ami(e)* m/f a·mee
from *de* der
frozen *gelé(e)* m/f zher·lay
fruit *fruit* m frwee
fry *faire frire* fair freer
frying pan *poêle* f pwal
full *plein(e)* m/f plun/plen
funny *drôle* m/f drol
furniture *meubles* m pl mer·bler

G

game (football) *match* m matsh
garbage can *poubelle* f poo·bel
garden *jardin* m zhar·dun
gas (for cooking) *gaz* m gaz
gas (petrol) *essence* f ay·sons
gastroenteritis *gastro-entérite* f gastro·on·tay·reet
gay *homosexuel(le)* m/f o·mo·sek·swel
Germany *Allemagne* f al·ma·nyer
get off (a train, etc) *descendre* day·son·drer
gift *cadeau* m ka·do
gig *concert* m kon·sair
girl *fille* f fee·yer
girlfriend *petite amie* f per·teet a·mee
glass *verre* f vair
glasses (spectacles) *lunettes* f pl lew·net
gloves *gants* m pl gon
go *aller* a·lay
go out *sortir* sor·teer
gold *or* m or
golf course *terrain* m *de golf* tay·run der golf

good *bon/bonne* m/f bon/bon
goodbye *au revoir* o rer·vwar
gram *gramme* m gram
grandchild *petit-fils/petite-fille* m/f per·tee fees/per·teet fee·yer
grandfather *grand-père* m grom·pair
grandmother *grand-mère* m grom·mair
grapes *raisins* m pl ray·sun
grateful *reconnaissant(e)* m/f rer·ko·nay·son(t)
great (fantastic) *génial(e)* m/f zhay·nyal
grocery *épicerie* f ay·pee·sree
guaranteed *garanti(e)* m/f ga·ron·tee
guesthouse *pension* f *(de famille)* pon·syon (der fa·mee·yer)
guide (person) *guide* m geed
guidebook *guide* m geed
guided tour *visite* f *guidée* vee·zeet gee·day
gym *gymnase* m zheem·naz

H

haircut *coupe* f koop
hairdresser *coiffeur/coiffeuse* m/f kwa·fer/kwa·ferz
half *moitié* f mwa·tyay
hand *main* f mun
handbag *sac* m *à main* sak a mun
handicrafts *objets* m pl *artisanaux* ob·zhay ar·tee·za·no
handkerchief *mouchoir* m moo·shwar
handmade *fait/faite à la main* m/f fay/fet a la mun
handsome *beau/belle* m/f bo/bel
happy *heureux/heureuse* m/f er·rer/er·rerz
hard (not soft) *dur(e)* m/f dewr
hat *chapeau* m sha·po
have *avoir* a·vwar
hay fever *rhume* m *des foins* rewm day fwun
he *il* eel
head *tête* f tet
headache *mal* m *à la tête* mal a la tet
headlights *phares* m pl far

heart *cœur* m ker
heart condition *maladie* f *de cœur* ma·la·dee der ker
heat *chaleur* f sha·ler
heated *chauffé(e)* m/f sho·fay
heater *appareil* m *de chauffage* a·pa·ray der sho·fazh
heavy *lourd(e)* m/f loor(d)
help *aider* ay·day
help *aide* f ed
her *son/sa/ses* m/f/pl son/sa/say
here *ici* ee·see
high *haut(e)* m/f o(t)
highway *autoroute* f o·to·root
hike *faire la randonnée* fair la ron·do·nay
hiking *randonnée* f ron·do·nay
hire *louer* loo·ay
his *son/sa/ses* m/f/pl son/sa/say
hitchhike *faire du stop* fair dew stop
holidays *vacances* f pl va·kons
home *à la maison* a la may·zon
homosexual *homosexuel(le)* m/f o·mo·sek·swel
honeymoon *lune* f *de miel* lewn der myel
horse riding *équitation* f ay·kee·ta·syon
hospital *hôpital* m o·pee·tal
hot *chaud(e)* m/f sho(d)
hotel *hôtel* m o·tel
hour *heure* f er
hungry (to be) *avoir faim* a·vwar fum
husband *mari* m ma·ree

I

I *je* zher
ice *glace* f glas
ice cream *glace* f glas
identification card (ID) *carte* f *d'identité* kart dee·don·tee·tay
ill *malade* ma·lad
important *important(e)* m/f um·por·ton(t)
impossible *impossible* um·po·see·bler
in *dans* don

in a hurry *pressé(e)* m/f pray·say
included *compris(e)* m/f kom·pree(z)
indigestion *indigestion* f un·dee·zhes·tyon
infection *infection* f un·fek·syon
influenza *grippe* f greep
information *renseignements* m pl ron·sen·yer·mon
injection *piqûre* f pee·kewr
injured *blessé(e)* m/f blay·say
injury *blessure* f blay·sewr
insurance *assurance* f a·sew·rons
intermission *entracte* m on·trakt
Internet *Internet* m un·tair·net
Internet café *cybercafé* m see·bair·ka·fay
interpreter *interprète* m/f un·tair·pret
Ireland *Irlande* f eer·lond
iron (for clothes) *fer* m *à repasser* fair a rer·pa·say
island *île* f eel
IT *informatique* f un·for·ma·teek
Italy *Italie* f ee·ta·lee
itch *démangeaison* f day·mon·zhay·zon
itinerary *itinéraire* m ee·tee·nay·rair

J

jacket *veste* f vest
jam *confiture* f kon·fee·tewr
jeans *jean* m zheen
jet lag *fatigue* f *due au décalage horaire* fa·teeg dew o day·ka·lazh o·rair
jewellery *bijoux* m pl bee·zhoo
job *travail* m tra·vai
journey *voyage* m vwa·yazh
jumper (sweater) *pull* m pewl

K

key *clé* f klay
kilo *kilo* m kee·lo
kilogram *kilogramme* m kee·lo·gram
kilometre *kilomètre* m kee·lo·may·trer

kind (nice) *gentil(le)* m/f zhon·tee
kiosk *kiosque* m kyosk
kitchen *cuisine* f kwee·zeen
knee *genou* m zhnoo
knife *couteau* m koo·to

L

lake *lac* m lak
lamb *agneau* m a·nyo
language *langue* f longk
laptop *ordinateur* m *portable*
  or·dee·na·ter por·ta·bler
last (previous) *dernier/dernière* m/f
  dair·nyay/dair·nyair
late *en retard* on rer·tar
later *plus tard* plew·tar
launderette *laverie* f lav·ree
laundry (place) *blanchisserie* f
  blon·shees·ree
laundry (clothes) *linge* m lunzh
law (study, professsion) *droit* m drwa
lawyer *avocat(e)* m/f a·vo·ka(t)
laxative *laxatif* m lak·sa·teef
leather *cuir* m kweer
left (direction) *à gauche* a gosh
left luggage (office) *consigne* f kon·see·nyer
leg *jambe* f zhomb
lemon *citron* m pl see·tron
lens *objectif* m ob·zhek·teef
lesbian *lesbienne* f les·byen
less *moins* mwun
letter *lettre* f lay·trer
lettuce *laitue* f lay·tew
library *bibliothèque* f bee·blee·o·tek
life jacket *gilet* m *de sauvetage* zhee·lay
  der sov·tazh
lift (elevator) *ascenseur* m a·son·ser
light *lumière* f lew·myair
light (not heavy) *léger/légère* m/f
  lay·zhay/lay·zhair
light (of colour) *clair(e)* m/f klair
light meter *posemètre* m poz·may·trer

lighter *briquet* m bree·kay
like *comme* kom
linen (material) *lin* m lun
linen (sheets etc) *linge* m lunzh
lipstick *rouge* m *à lèvres* roozh a lay·vrer
liquor store *magasin* m *de vins et spiritueux*
  ma·ga·zun der vun ay spee·ree·twer
listen (to) *écouter* ay·koo·tay
little bit *peu* m per
lobster *homard* m o·mar
local *local(e)* m/f lo·kal
lock *fermer à clé* fair·may a klay
locked *fermé(e) à clé* m/f fair·may a klay
long *long(ue)* m/f long(k)
lost *perdu(e)* m/f pair·dew
lost property office *bureau* m *des objets*
  trouvés bew·ro day zob·zhay troo·vay
loud *fort(e)* m/f for(t)
love *amour* a·moor
love *aimer* ay·may
lubricant *lubrifiant* m lew·bree·fyon
luggage *bagages* m pl ba·gazh
luggage lockers *consigne* f *automatique*
  kon·see·nyer o·to·ma·teek
lunch *déjeuner* m day·zher·nay
luxury *de luxe* der lewks

M

mail (letters) *courrier* m koo·ryay
mail (postal system) *poste* f post
mailbox *boîte* f *aux lettres* bwat o lay·trer
make-up *maquillage* m ma·kee·yazh
man *homme* m om
manager (restaurant, hotel) *gérant(e)*
  m/f zhay·ron(t)
map (of country) *carte* f kart
map (of town) *plan* m plon
market *marché* m mar·shay
married *marié(e)* m/f ma·ryay
massage *massage* m ma·sazh
masseur/masseuse *masseur/masseuse*
  m/f ma·ser/ma·serz

match (sports) *match* m matsh
matches (for lighting) *allumettes* f pl
  a-lew-met
mattress *matelas* m mat-la
me *moi* mwa
meal *repas* m rer-pa
meat *viande* f vyond
medicine *médecine* f med-seen
medicine (medication) *médicament* m
  may-dee-ka-mon
menu *carte* kart
message *message* m may-sazh
metre *mètre* m may-trer
metro station *station* f *de métro* sta-syon
  der may-tro
microwave (oven) *four* m *à micro-ondes*
  foor a mee-kro-ond
midday/noon *midi* mee-dee
midnight *minuit* mee-nwee
milk *lait* m lay
millimetre *millimètre* m mee-lee-may-trer
mineral water *eau* f *minérale*
  o mee-nay-ral
minute *minute* f mee-newt
mirror *miroir* m mee-rwar
Miss *Mademoiselle* mad-mwa-zel
mobile phone *téléphone* m *portable*
  tay-lay-fon por-ta-bler
modem *modem* m mo-dem
modern *moderne* mo-dairn
money *argent* m ar-zhon
month *mois* m mwa
more *plus* plew
morning *matin* m ma-tun
motel *motel* m mo-tel
mother *mère* f mair
motorcycle *moto* f mo-to
motorway (tollway) *autoroute* f o-to-root
mountain *montagne* f mon-ta-nyer
mouth *bouche* f boosh
movie *film* m feelm
Mr *Monsieur* mer-syer
Mrs *Madame* ma-dam

Ms *Mademoiselle* mad-mwa-zel
museum *musée* m mew-zay
muesli *muesli* m mewz-lee
music *musique* f mew-zeek
music shop *disquaire* m dee-skair
my *mon/ma/mes* m/f/pl mon/ma/may

N

nail clippers *coupe-ongles* m koop-ong-gler
name (general) *nom* m nom
name (first/given) *prénom* m pray-non
napkin *serviette* f sair-vyet
nappy *couche* f koosh
nausea *nausée* f no-zay
near *près* de pray der
nearby *tout près* too pray
nearest *le/la plus proche* m/f ler/la plew
  prosh
necklace *collier* m ko-lyay
needle *aiguille* f ay-gwee-yer
Netherlands *Pays-Bas* m pl pay-ee-ba
new *nouveau/nouvelle* m/f noo-vo/
  noo-vel
New Year's Day *jour de l'An* zhoor der lon
New Year's Eve *Saint-Sylvestre* f
  sun-seel-ves-trer
New Zealand *Nouvelle-Zélande* f
  noo-vel-zay-lond
news *les nouvelles* lay noo-vel
newsagent *marchand* m *de journaux*
  mar-shon der zhoor-no
newspaper *journal* m zhoor-nal
next (month, etc) *prochain(e)* m/f
  pro-shun/pro-shen
night *nuit* f nwee
night out *soirée* f swa-ray
nightclub *boîte* f bwat
no vacancy *complet* kom-play
no *non* non
noisy *bruyant(e)* m/f brew-yon(t)
nonsmoking *non-fumeur* non-few-mer
north *nord* m nor

nose *nez* m nay
notebook *carnet* m kar·nay
nothing *rien* ryun
now *maintenant* mun·ter·non
number *numéro* m new·may·ro
nurse *infirmier/infirmière* m/f
  un·feer·myay/un·feer·myair
nut *noix* f nwa

O

off (spoiled) *mauvais(e)* m/f mo·vay(z)
oil *huile* f weel
oil (petrol) *pétrole* m pay·trol
old *vieux/vieille* m/f vyer/vyay
on *sur* sewr
onion *oignon* m o·nyon
on time *à l'heure* a ler
one *un(e)* m/f un/ewn
one-way (ticket) *(billet) simple* (bee·yay)
  sum·pler
open *ouvert(e)* m/f oo·vair(t)
open *ouvrir* oo·vreer
opening hours *heures* f pl *d'ouverture*
  er doo·vair·tewr
optometrist *optométriste* m&f
  op·to·may·treest
orange *orange* o·ronzh
other *autre* o·trer
our *notre* no·trer
outside *dehors* der·or
overnight *pendant la nuit*
  pon·don la nwee
overseas *outre-mer* oo·trer·mair
oysters *huîtres* f pl wee·trer

P

pacifier (dummy) *tétine* f tay·teen
package *paquet* m pa·kay
packet (general) *paquet* m pa·kay
padlock *cadenas* m kad·na

pain *douleur* f doo·ler
painful *douloureux/douloureuse* m/f
  doo·loo·rer/doo·loo·rerz
painkiller *analgésique* m a·nal·zhay·zeek
painter *peintre* m pun·trer
painting (a work) *tableau* m ta·blo
painting (the art) *peinture* f pun·tewr
palace *palais* m pa·lay
pants *pantalon* m pon·ta·lon
panty liners *protège-slips* m pl
  pro·tezh·sleep
pantyhose *collant* m ko·lon
paper *papier* m pa·pyay
paperwork *paperasserie* f pa·pras·ree
parcel *colis* m ko·lee
parents *parents* m pl pa·ron
park *parc* m park
park (a car) *garer (une voiture)* ga·ray
  (ewn vwa·tewr)
party (night out) *soirée* f swa·ray
passenger *voyageur/voyageuse* m/f
  vwa·ya·zher/vwa·ya·zherz
passport *passeport* m pas·por
passport number *numéro* m *de passeport*
  new·may·ro der pas·por
path *chemin* m shmun
payment *paiement* m pay·mon
peach *pêche* f pesh
pear *poire* f pwar
pen (ballpoint) *stylo* m stee·lo
pencil *crayon* m kray·yon
penis *pénis* m pay·nees
penknife *canif* m ka·neef
pensioner *retraité(e)* m/f rer·tray·tay
pepper (bell) *poivron* m pwa·vron
perfume *parfum* m par·fum
petrol *essence* f ay·sons
petrol station *station-service* f
  sta·syon·sair·vees
pharmacy *pharmacie* f far·ma·see
phone book *annuaire* m an·wair
phone box *cabine* f *téléphonique* ka·been
  tay·lay·fo·neek

phone card *télécarte* f tay-lay-kart
photo *photo* f fo-to
photograph *prendre en photo* pron-drer on fo-to
photographer *photographe* m/f fo-to-graf
photography *photographie* f fo-to-gra-fee
phrasebook *recueil m d'expressions* rer-ker-yer dek-spray-syon
picnic *pique-nique* m peek-neek
pill *pilule* f pee-lewl
pillow *oreiller* m o-ray-yay
pillowcase *taie f d'oreiller* tay do-ray-yay
plane *avion* m a-vyon
plate *assiette* f a-syet
platform *quai* m kay
play (theatre) *pièce f de théâtre* pyes der tay-a-trer
plug (bath) *bonde* f bond
plug (electricity) *prise* f preez
plum *prune* f • *mirabelle* f prewn • mee-ra-bel
point *indiquer* un-dee-kay
police *police* f po-lees
police officer (in city) *policier* m po-lee-syay
police officer (in country) *gendarme* m zhon-darm
police station *commissariat* m ko-mee-sar-ya
pool (swimming) *piscine* f pee-seen
pork *porc* m por
post code *code m postal* kod pos-tal
post office *bureau m de poste* bew-ro der post
postcard *carte postale* f kart pos-tal
potato *pomme f de terre* pom der tair
pound (money, weight) *livre* f leev-rer
prawns *crevettes f pl roses* kre-vet roz
pregnant *enceinte* on-sunt
prescription *ordonnance* f or-do-nons
present (gift) *cadeau* m ka-do
price *prix* m pree

printer (computer) *imprimante* f um-pree-mont
private *privé(e)* m/f pree-vay
prostitute *prostituée* f pro-stee-tway
pub (bar) *bar* m bar
public telephone *téléphone m public* tay-lay-fon pewb-leek
public toilet *toilettes* f pl twa-let
purse *porte-monnaie* m port-mo-nay

Q

quiet *tranquille* trong-keel

R

radio *radio* f ra-dyo
railway station *gare* f gar
rain *pluie* f plwee
raincoat *imperméable* m um-pair-may-abler
rare *rare* rar
raspberry *framboise* f from-bwaz
rave *rave* f raiv
razor *rasoir* m ra-zwar
razor blade *lame f de rasoir* lam der ra-zwar
rear (seat etc) *arrière* a-ryair
receipt *reçu* m rer-sew
recommend *recommander* rer-ko-mon-day
refrigerator *réfrigérateur* m ray-free-zhay-ra-ter
refund *remboursement* m rom-boor-ser-mon
registered mail/post (by) *en recommandé* on rer-ko-mon-day
remote control *télécommande* f tay-lay-ko-mond
rent *louer* loo-ay
repair *réparer* ray-pa-ray
reservation *réservation* f ray-zair-va-syon

restaurant *restaurant* m res·to·ron
return (come back) *revenir* rerv·neer
return (ticket) *aller retour* m a·lay rer·toor
right (direction) *à droite* a drwat
ring (on finger) *bague* f bag
river *rivière* f ree·vyair
road *route* f root
romantic *romantique* ro·mon·teek
room *chambre* f shom·brer
room number *numéro* m *de chambre* new·may·ro der shom·brer
ruins *ruines* f pl rween

S

safe *coffre-fort* m kof·rer·for
safe sex *rapports* m pl *sexuels protégés* ra·por seks·wel pro·tay·zhay
sanitary napkin *serviette* f *hygiénique* sair·vyet ee·zhyay·neek
scarf *écharpe* f ay·sharp
science *science* f syons
scientist *scientifique* m/f syon·tee·feek
scissors *ciseaux* m pl see·zo
Scotland *Écosse* f ay·kos
sculpture *sculpture* f skewl·tewr
sea *mer* f mair
seafood *fruits* m pl *de mer* frwee der mair
season *saison* f say·zon
seat (place) *place* f plas
seatbelt *ceinture* f *de sécurité* sun·tewr der say·kew·ree·tay
second class *de seconde classe* der skond klas
self service *libre-service* m lee·brer·sair·vees
service *service* m sair·vees
service charge *service* m sair·vees
service station *station-service* f sta·syon·sair·vees
sex *sexe* m seks
shade *ombre* f om·brer

share (a dorm etc) *partager* par·ta·zhay
share (with) *partager (avec)* par·ta·zhay (a·vek)
shave *se raser* ser ra·zay
shaving cream *mousse* f *à raser* moos a ra·zay
sheet (bed) *drap* m dra
shirt *chemise* f sher·meez
shoe *chaussure* f sho·sewr
shoe shop *magasin* m *de chaussures* ma·ga·zun der sho·sewr
shop *magasin* m ma·ga·zun
shop *faire des courses* fair day koors
shopping centre *centre* m *commercial* son·trer ko·mair·syal
short (height) *court(e)* m/f koor(t)
shorts *short* m short
shoulder *épaule* f ay·pol
show *spectacle* m spek·ta·kler
show *montrer* mon·tray
shower *douche* f doosh
shrimps *crevettes* f pl *grises* kre·vet grees
shut *fermé(e)* m/f fair·may
sick *malade* ma·lad
silk *soie* f swa
silver *argent* m ar·zhon
single (person) *célibataire* say·lee·ba·tair
single room *chambre* f *pour une personne* shom·brer poor ewn pair·son
sister *sœur* f ser
size (general) *taille* f tai
skiing *ski* m skee
skirt *jupe* f zhewp
sleep *dormir* dor·meer
sleeping bag *sac* m *de couchage* sak der koo·shazh
sleeping car *wagon-lit* m va·gon·lee
slice *tranche* f tronsh
slide (film) *diapositive* f dya·po·zee·teev
slowly *lentement* lon·ter·mon
small *petit(e)* m/f per·tee/per·teet
smaller *plus petit(e)* m/f plew per·tee/·teet

LOOK UP

smallest *le plus petit/la plus petite* m/f
ler plew per·tee/la plew per·teet
smell *odeur* f o·der
smoke *fumer* few·may
snack *casse-croûte* m kas·kroot
snow *neige* f nezh
soap *savon* m sa·von
socks *chaussettes* f sho·set
some *du/de la/des* m/f/pl dew/der la/day
son *fils* m fees
soon *bientôt* byun·to
south *sud* m sewd
souvenir *souvenir* m soov·neer
souvenir shop *magasin* m *de souvenirs*
ma·ga·zun der soov·neer
Spain *Espagne* f es·pa·nyer
speak *parler* par·lay
speed limit *limitation* f *de vitesse*
lee·mee·ta·syon der vee·tes
spinach *épinards* m pl ay·pee·nar
spoon *cuillère* f kwee·yair
sports store/shop *magasin* m *de sports*
ma·ga·zun der spor
sprain *entorse* f on·tors
spring (season) *printemps* m prun·tom
square (town) *place* f plas
stairway *escalier* m es·ka·lyay
stamp *timbre* m tum·brer
stand-by ticket *billet* m *stand-by* bee·yay
stond·bai
station *gare* f gar
stationer's (shop) *papeterie* f pa·pet·ree
stockings *bas* m ba
stolen *volé(e)* m/f vo·lay
stomach *estomac* m es·to·ma
stomachache (to have a) *avoir mal au*
ventre a·vwar mal o von·trer
Stop! *Arrêtez!* a·ray·tay
strawberry *fraise* f frez
street *rue* f rew
street market *braderie* f bra·dree
strike *grève* f grev

stroller *poussette* f poo·set
student *étudiant(e)* m/f ay·tew·dyon(t)
subtitles *sous-titres* m pl soo·tee·trer
subway *métro* m may·tro
suitcase *valise* f va·leez
summer *été* m ay·tay
sun *soleil* m so·lay
sunblock *écran* m *solaire total* ay·kron
so·lair to·tal
sunburn *coup* m *de soleil* koo der so·lay
sunglasses *lunettes* f *de soleil* lew·net
der so·lay
sunrise *lever* m *du soleil* ler·vay dew
so·lay
sunset *coucher* m *du soleil* koo·shay
dew so·lay
supermarket *supermarché* m
sew·pair·mar·shay
surface mail (land) *voie* f *de terre* vwa
der tair
surface mail (sea) *voie* f *maritime* vwa
ma·ree·teem
surname *nom* m *de famille* nom der
fa·mee·yer
sweater *pull* m pewl
sweet *sucré(e)* m/f sew·kray
swim *nager* na·zhay
swimming pool *piscine* f pee·seen
swimsuit *maillot* m *de bain* ma·yo der bun

T

tailor *tailleur* m ta·yer
tampon *tampon* m *hygiénique* tom·pon
ee·zhyay·neek
tanning lotion *crème* f *de bronzage* krem
der bron·zazh
tap *robinet* m ro·bee·nay
tasty *délicieux/délicieuse* m/f day·lees·yer/
day·lees·yerz
taxi *taxi* m tak·see

taxi stand *station f de taxi* sta·syon der tak·see
teacher *professeur* m pro·fay·ser
teaspoon *petite cuillère* f per·teet kwee·yair
telegram *télégramme* m tay·lay·gram
telephone *téléphone* m tay·lay·fon
telephone *téléphoner* tay·lay·fo·nay
telephone box *cabine f téléphonique* ka·been tay·lay·fo·neek
television *télé(vision)* f tay·lay(vee·zyon)
temperature *température* f tom·pay·ra·tewr
tennis *tennis* m tay·nees
tennis court *court m de tennis* koor der tay·nees
thank you *merci* mair·see
that (one) *cela* ser·la
theatre *théâtre* m tay·a·trer
there *là* la
thirsty (to be) *avoir soif* a·vwar swaf
this (one) *ceci* ser·see
throat *gorge* f gorzh
ticket *billet* m bee·yay
ticket machine *distributeur m de tickets* dee·stree·bew·ter der tee·kay
ticket office *guichet* m gee·shay
time *temps* m tom
time difference *décalage m horaire* day·ka·lazh o·rair
timetable *horaire* m o·rair
tin (can) *boîte* f bwat
tin opener *ouvre-boîte* m oo·vrer·bwat
tip (gratuity) *pourboire* m poor·bwar
tire *pneu* m pner
tired *fatigué(e)* m/f fa·tee·gay
tissues *mouchoirs m en papier* moo·shwar om pa·pyay
to *à* a
toast *pain grillé* m pun gree·yay
toaster *grille-pain* m greey·pun
today *aujourd'hui* o·zhoor·dwee
together *ensemble* on·som·bler

toilet *toilettes* f pl twa·let
toilet paper *papier m hygiénique* pa·pyay ee·zhyay·neek
tomato *tomate* f to·mat
tomorrow *demain* der·mun
tomorrow afternoon *demain après-midi* der·mun a·pray·mee·dee
tomorrow evening *demain soir* der·mun swar
tomorrow morning *demain matin* der·mum ma·tun
tonight *ce soir* ser swar
too (expensive etc) *trop* tro
toothache *mal m de dents* mal der don
toothbrush *brosse f à dents* bros a don
toothpaste *dentifrice* m don·tee·frees
torch (flashlight) *lampe f de poche* lomp der posh
tour *voyage* m vwa·yazh
tourist office *office de tourisme* m o·fees·der too·rees·mer
towel *serviette* f sair·vyet
train *train* m trun
train station *gare* f gar
transit lounge *salle f de transit* sal der tron·zeet
translate *traduire* tra·dweer
travel agency *agence f de voyage* a·zhons der vwa·yazh
travel sickness *mal m des transports* mal day trons·por
travellers cheque *chèque m de voyage* shek der vwa·yazh
trolley *chariot* m shar·yo
trousers *pantalon* m pon·ta·lon
try *essayer* ay·say·yay
T-shirt *T-shirt* m tee·shert
TV *télé* f tay·lay
tweezers *pince f à épiler* puns a ay·pee·lay
twin beds *lits m pl jumeaux* lee zhew·mo
two *deux* der
tyre *pneu* m pner

U

umbrella *parapluie* m pa·ra·plwee
uncomfortable *inconfortable*
ung·kon·for·ta·bler
underwear *sous-vêtements* m
soo·vet·mon
university *université* f
ew·nee·vair·see·tay
until (eg, Friday) *jusqu'à* zhew·ska
up *en haut* o
urgent *urgent(e)* m/f ewr·zhon(t)
USA *les États Unis* m pl lay zay·taz ew·nee

V

vacancy *chambre* f *libre* shom·brer
lee·brer
vacant *libre* lee·brer
vacation *vacances* f pl va·kons
vaccination *vaccination* f vak·see·na·syon
validate *valider* va·lee·day
valuable *de valeur* der va·ler
veal *veau* m vo
vegetable *légume* m lay·gewm
vegetarian *végétarien/végétarienne* m/f
vay·zhay·ta·ryun/vay·zhay·ta·ryen
video recorder *magnétoscope* m
ma·nyay·to·skop
video tape *bande* f *vidéo* bond vee·day·o
view *vue* f vew
visa *visa* m vee·za

W

wait (for) *attendre* a·ton·drer
waiter *serveur/serveuse* m/f
sair·ver/sair·verz
waiting room *salle* f *d'attente* sal da·tont
wake (someone) up *réveiller* ray·vay·yay
Wales *Pays de Galle* m pay der gal
walk *marcher* mar·shay

warm *chaud(e)* m/f sho(d)
wash (something) *laver* la·vay
washing machine *machine* f *à laver*
ma·sheen a la·vay
watch *montre* f mon·trer
water *eau* f o
water bottle (hot) *bouillotte* f boo·yot
week *semaine* f ser·men
weekend *week-end* m week·end
west *ouest* m west
wheelchair *fauteuil* m *roulant* fo·ter·yee
roo·lon
when *quand* kon
where *où* oo
which *quel(le)* m/f kel
white *blanc/blanche* m/f blong/blonsh
who *qui* kee
why *pourquoi* poor·kwa
wife *femme* f fam
window *fenêtre* f fer·nay·trer
wine *vin* m vun
winter *hiver* m ee·vair
without *sans* son
woman *femme* f fam
wool *laine* f len
write *écrire* ay·kreer

Y

year *année* m a·nay
yes *oui* wee
yesterday *hier* ee·yair
you sg pol & pl *vous* voo
you inf *tu* tew
youth hostel *auberge* f *de jeunesse*
o·bairzh der zher·nes

Z

zip/zipper *fermeture* f *éclair* fair·mer·tewr
ay·klair
zoo *zoo* m zo

A French–English dictionary

Nouns in this dictionary have their gender indicated by m (masculine) or f (feminine).
If it's a plural noun, you'll also see pl.
Where no gender is marked the word is either an adjective or a verb, with adjectives first.

A

auto m o·to *car*
à a *at*
acheter ash·tay *buy*
addition f a·dee·syon *bill (restaurant) •
check (bill)*
aéroport m a·ay·ro·por *airport*
affaires f pl a·fair *business*
agence f de voyage a·zhons der
vwa·yazh *travel agency*
agence f immobilière a·zhons
ee·mo·bee·lyair *estate agency*
aider ay·day *help*
alcool m al·kol *alcohol*
aller a·lay *go*
aller retour m a·lay rer·toor *return (ticket)*
ambassade f om·ba·sad *embassy*
amende f a·mond *fine (penalty)*
ami(e) m/f a·mee *friend*
anglais(e) m/f ong·glay(z) *English*
année f a·nay *year*
anniversaire m a·nee·vair·sair *birthday*
annuaire m an·wair *phone book*
annuler a·new·lay *cancel*
antiquité f on·tee·kee·tay *antique*
appareil m photo a·pa·ray fo·to *camera*
appeler a·per·lay *call*
après-demain a·pray·der·mun *day after
tomorrow (the)*
après-midi a·pray·mee·dee *afternoon*
argent m ar·zhon *money • silver*
arrêt m d'autobus a·ray do·to·bews
bus stop
arrivées f pl a·ree·vay *arrivals*
artisanat m ar·tee·za·na *crafts*
ascenseur m a·son·ser *lift • elevator*

assez a·say *enough*
assurance f a·sew·rons *insurance*
Attention! a·ton·syon *Careful!*
auberge f de jeunesse o·bairzh der
zher·nes *youth hostel*
aujourd'hui o·zhoor·dwee *today*
automne m o·ton *fall (autumn)*
autoroute f o·to·root *highway • motorway
(tollway)*
avant-hier a·von·tyair *day before
yesterday (the)*
avion m a·vyon *aeroplane*

B

bac m bak *ferry*
bagages m pl ba·gazh *luggage*
baignoire f be·nywar *bath*
banque f bonk *bank*
bateau m ba·to *boat*
bâtiment m ba·tee·mon *building*
beau/belle m/f bo/bel *beautiful*
bébé m bay·bay *baby*
bientôt byun·to *soon*
bière f byair *beer*
bijoux m pl bee·zhoo *jewellery*
billet m bee·yay *ticket*
— **simple** sum·pler *one-way (ticket)*
blan(che) m/f blon(sh) *white*
bleu(e) m/f bler *blue*
boire bwar *drink*
boisson f bwa·son *drink*
boîte f bwat *box • nightclub*
boucherie f boosh·ree *butcher's shop*
boulangerie f boo·lon·zhree *bakery*
bouteille f boo·tay *bottle*
briquet m bree·kay *cigarette lighter*
brun/brune m/f brun/brewn *brown*

bureau m bew·ro *office*
— **de poste** der post *post office*
— **des objets trouvés** day zob·zhay troo·vay *lost property office*
(auto)bus m (o·to)bews *bus (city)*

C

cabine f **téléphonique** ka·been tay·lay·fo·neek *phone box*
cadeau m ka·do *present (gift)*
café m ka·fay *coffee* • *café*
caissier/caissière m/f kay·syay/kay·syair *cashier*
campagne f kom·pa·nyer *countryside*
canif m ka·neef *penknife*
(auto)car m (o·to)kar *bus (intercity)*
carte f kart *menu* • *map (of country)*
— **d'embarquement** dom·bar·ker·mon *boarding pass*
— **d'identité** dee·don·tee·tay *identification card (ID)*
— **de crédit** der kray·dee *credit card*
— **grise** greez *car owner's title*
— **postale** pos·tal *postcard*
cassé(e) m/f ka·say *broken*
casse-croûte m kas·kroot *snack*
ceinture f **de sécurité** sun·tewr der say·kew·ree·tay *seatbelt*
célibataire m say·lee·ba·tair *single (person)*
cendrier m son·dree·yay *ashtray*
centre m **commercial** son·trer ko·mair·syal *shopping centre*
centre-ville m son·trer·veel *city centre*
chambre f shom·brer *room*
— **à coucher** a koo·shay *bedroom*
— **libre** lee·brer *vacancy*
— **pour deux personnes** poor der pair·son *double room*
— **pour une personne** poor ewn pair·son *single room*

changer shon·zhay *change*
chaque shak *each* • *every*
chaud(e) m/f sho(d) *hot* • *warm*
chauffé(e) m/f sho·fay *heated*
chaussettes f sho·set *socks*
chaussure f sho·sewr *shoe*
chemin m shmun *path*
chemise f sher·meez *shirt*
chèque m shek *check (banking)* • *cheque*
— **de voyage** der vwa·yazh *travellers cheque*
cher/chère m/f shair *expensive*
chien m shyun *dog*
cimetière m seem·tyair *cemetery*
cirque m seerk *circus*
classe f **affaires** klas a·fair *business class*
classe f **touriste** klas too·reest *economy class*
clé f klay *key*
climatisé(e) m/f kee·ma·tee·zay *air-conditioned*
code m **postal** kod pos·tal *post code*
coffre-fort m kof·rer·for *safe*
collant m ko·lon *pantyhose*
commissariat m ko·mee·sar·ya *police station*
complet kom·play *no vacancy*
complet/complète m/f kom·play/kom·plet *booked up*
compris(e) m/f kom·pree(z) *included*
compte m kont *account*
— **bancaire** bong·kair *bank account*
confirmer kon·feer·may *confirm (a booking)*
confortable kon·for·ta·bler *comfortable*
consigne f kon·see·nyer *left luggage (office)*
— **automatique** o·to·ma·teek *luggage lockers*
couche f koosh *nappy* • *diaper*
court(e) m/f koor(t) *short (height)*

couvert m koo·vair *cover charge*
couverture f koo·vair·tewr *blanket*
cuir m kweer *leather*
cuisine f kwee·zeen *kitchen*
cuisinier/cuisinière m/f kwee·zee·nyay/
kwee·zee·nyair *cook*
cybercafé m see·bair·ka·fay *Internet cafe*

D

date f de naissance dat der nay·sons
date of birth
déjeuner m day·zher·nay *lunch*
demain der·mun *tomorrow*
— après-midi a·pray·mee·dee
tomorrow afternoon
— matin ma·tun *tomorrow morning*
— soir swar *tomorrow evening*
départ m day·par *departure*
dépôt m day·po *deposit*
dernier/dernière m/f dair·nyay/
dair·nyair *last (previous)*
diapositive f dya·po·zee·teev *slide (film)*
dictionnaire m deek·syo·nair *dictionary*
dîner m dee·nay *dinner*
direct(e) m/f dee·rekt *direct*
disquaire m dee·skair *music shop*
disque m deesk *disk (CD-ROM)*
disquette f dees·ket *disk (floppy)*
distributeur m de tickets
dee·stree·bew·ter der tee·kay *ticket
machine*
doigt m dwa *finger*
dos m do *back (body)*
douane f dwan *customs*
douche f doosh *shower*
draps m dra *bed linen*

E

eau f o *water*
— minérale mee·nay·ral *mineral water*

échange m ay·shonzh *exchange*
échanger ay·shon·zhay *change (money)* ·
exchange
église f ay·gleez *church*
en retard on rer·tar *late*
enfant m/f on·fon *child*
enregistrement on·rer·zhee·strer·mon
check-in (desk)
ensemble on·som·bler *together*
entracte m on·trakt *intermission*
entrée m on·tray *entry*
entreprise f on·trer·preez *company*
enveloppe f on·vlop *envelope*
épicerie f ay·pee·sree *grocery*
escalier m es·ka·lyay *stairway*
essence f ay·sons *gasoline* · *petrol*
est m est *east*
étage m ay·tazh *floor (storey)*
été m ay·tay *summer*
étranger/étrangère m/f ay·tron·zhay/
ay·tron·zhair *foreign*
étudiant(e) m/f ay·tew·dyon(t) *student*
excédent ek·say·don *excess (baggage)*
exposition f ek·spo·zee·syon *exhibition*
(par) exprès eks·pres *express (mail)*

F

faire les courses fair lay koors *go shopping*
famille f fa·mee·yer *family*
félicitations fay·lee·see·ta·syon
congratulations
femme f fam *wife* · *woman*
fenêtre f fer·nay·trer *window*
fermé(e) m/f fair·may *closed*
— à clé m/f a klay *locked*
fièvre f fyev·rer *fever*
fille f fee·yer *daughter* · *girl*
fils m fees *son*
forêt f fo·ray *forest*
frais/fraîche m/f fray/fresh *fresh*

franchise f fron·sheez *baggage allowance*
freins m frun *brakes*
frère m frair *brother*
froid(e) m/f frwa(d) *cold*
frontière f fron·tyair *border*
fumer few·may *smoke*

G

gants m pl gon *gloves*
garçon m gar·son *boy*
gare f gar *train station*
— **routière** roo·tyair *bus station*
gaz m gaz *gas (for cooking)*
gendarme m zhon·darm *police officer (in country)*
gentil(le) m/f zhon·tee *kind (nice)*
grand(e) m/f gron(d) *big*
grand lit m gron lee *double bed*
grand magasin m gron ma·ga·zun *department store*
gratuit(e) m/f gra·twee(t) *free (gratis)*
grippe f greep *flu*
gris(e) m/f gree(z) *grey*
groupe m **sanguin** groop song·gun *blood group*
guichet m gee·shay *ticket office*
— **automatique de banque (GAB)** o·to·ma·teek der bonk *automatic teller machine (ATM)*

H

heure f er *hour*
heures f pl **d'ouverture** er doo·vair·tewr *opening hours*
hier ee·yair *yesterday*
hiver m ee·vair *winter*
homme m om *man*
hôpital m o·pee·tal *hospital*
horaire m o·rair *timetable*
hors service or sair·vees *out of order*
hôtel m o·tel *hotel*
huile f weel *oil*

I

ici ee·see *here*
immatriculation ee·ma·tree·kew·la·syon *car registration*
interprète m/f un·tair·pret *interpreter*
itinéraire m ee·tee·nay·rair *itinerary*
ivre ee·vrer *drunk*

J

jardin m zhar·dun *garden*
jean m zheen *jeans*
jour m zhoor *day*
journal m zhoor·nal *newspaper*
jupe f zhewp *skirt*

L

laine f len *wool*
lait m lay *milk*
laver la·vay *wash (something)*
laverie f lav·ree *launderette*
légume m lay·gewm *vegetable*
lettre f lay·trer *letter*
librairie f lee·bray·ree *bookshop*
libre m/f lee·brer *vacant*
libre-service m lee·brer·sair·vees *self service*
lin m lun *linen (material)*
linge m lunzh *laundry (clothes)*
lit m lee *bed*
lits m pl **jumeaux** lee zhew·mo *twin beds*
livre m leev·rer *book*
livre f leev·rer *pound (money, weight)*
location f **de voitures** lo·ka·syon der vwa·tewr *car hire*
logement m lozh·mon *accommodation*
louer loo·ay *hire · rent*
lune f **de miel** lewn der myel *honeymoon*
lunettes f pl lew·net *glasses (spectacles)*

M

machine f **à laver** ma·sheen a la·vay washing machine
magasin m ma·ga·zun shop
magnétoscope m ma·nyay·to·skop video recorder
maintenant mun·ter·non now
malade ma·lad sick
manger mon·zhay eat
manteau m mon·to coat
maquillage m ma·kee·yazh make-up
marchand m **de journaux** mar·shon der zhoor·no newsagent
marché m mar·shay market
— **aux puces** o pews fleamarket
marcher mar·shay walk
mari m ma·ree husband
matin m ma·tun morning
mauvais(e) m/f mo·vay(z) bad
médecin m mayd·sun doctor
médicament m may·dee·ka·mon medicine (medication)
mer f mair sea
mère f mair mother
midi m mee·dee midday • noon
minuit f mee·nwee midnight
mode f mod fashion
modem m mo·dem modem
mois m mwa month
moitié f mwa·tyay half
monnaie f mo·nay change (coins)
montagne f mon·ta·nyer mountain
montre f mon·trer watch
moto f mo·to motorcycle
musée m mew·zay art gallery • museum

N

nager na·zhay swim
neige f nezh snow
nettoyage m net·wa·yazh cleaning
nettoyer net·wa·yay clean
Noël m no·el Christmas

noir et blanc nwar ay blong B&W (film)
noir(e) m/f nwar black
nom m nom name
— **de famille** der fa·mee·yer surname
non-fumeur non·few·mer nonsmoking
nord m nor north
nuit f nwee night
numéro m new·may·ro number
— **de chambre** der shom·brer room number
— **de passeport** der pas·por passport number

O

occupé(e) m/f o·kew·pay busy
office de tourisme o·fees·der too·rees·mer tourist office
or m or gold
orange f o·ronzh orange
ordinateur m or·dee·na·ter computer
— **portable** por·ta·bler laptop
ordonnance f or·do·nons prescription
oreiller m o·ray·yay pillow
où oo where
ouest m west west
ouvert(e) m/f oo·vair(t) open

P

pain m pun bread
palais m pa·lay palace
pantalon m pon·ta·lon pants • trousers
papeterie f pa·pet·ree stationer's (shop)
papier m pa·pyay paper
partager par·ta·zhay share (a dorm etc)
partir par·teer depart (leave)
passeport m pas·por passport
peintre m pun·trer painter
peinture f pun·tewr painting (the art)
pellicule f pay·lee·kewl film (for camera)
pension f pon·syon boarding house
— **de famille** der fa·mee·yer guesthouse

French–English dictionary Q

perdu(e) m/f pair·dew *lost*

père m pair *father*

permis m **de conduire** pair·mee der kon·dweer *driver's licence*

petit ami m per·tee a·mee *boyfriend*

petit déjeuner m per·tee day·zher·nay *breakfast*

petite amie f per·teet a·mee *girlfriend*

pièce f **d'identité** pyes dee·don·tee·tay *identification*

pièce f **de théâtre** pyes der tay·a·trer *play (theatre)*

pièces f pl pyes *coins*

pile f peel *battery*

pique-nique m peek·neek *picnic*

piscine f pee·seen *swimming pool*

place f plas *seat (place)* • *square (town)*

plage f plazh *beach*

plan m plon *map (of town)*

plat m pla *dish*

plus tard plew·tar *later*

poissonnerie f pwa·son·ree *fish shop*

policier m po·lee·syay *police officer (in city)*

poste f post *mail (postal system)*

pourboire m poor·bwar *tip (gratuity)*

pourquoi poor·kwa *why*

première classe f prer·myair klas *first class*

prénom m pray·non *Christian name*

préservatif m pray·zair·va·teef *condom*

printemps m prun·tom *spring (season)*

prix m pree *price*

prochain(e) m/f pro·shun/pro·shen *next (month)*

pull m pewl *jumper (sweater)*

Q

quai m kay *platform*

quand kon *when*

quel(le) m/f kel *which*

qui kee *who*

quotidien(ne) m/f ko·tee·dyun/ ko·tee·dyen *daily*

R

rapide ra·peed *fast*

rapport m ra·por *connection*

reconnaissant(e) m/f rer·ko·nay·son(t) *grateful*

reçu m rer·sew *receipt*

recueil m **d'expressions** rer·ker·yer dek·spray·syon *phrasebook*

remboursement m rom·boor·ser·mon *refund*

remise f rer·meez *discount*

rendez-vous m ron·day·voo *appointment*

renseignements m pl ron·sen·yer·mon *information*

réparer ray·pa·ray *repair*

repas m rer·pa *meal*

réserver ray·zair·vay *book (make a booking)*

retard m rer·tard *delay*

retrait m **des bagages** rer·tray day ba·gazh *baggage claim*

retraité(e) m/f rer·tray·tay *pensioner*

réveil m ray·vay *alarm clock*

revenir rerv·neer *return (come back)*

robe f rob *dress*

rose roz *pink*

rouge roozh *red*

route f root *road*

rue f rew *street*

S

sac m sak *bag*

 — **à dos** a do *backpack*

 — **de couchage** der koo·shazh *sleeping bag*

saison f say·zon *season*

sale sal *dirty*

salle f sal *room*

 — **d'attente** da·tont *waiting room*

 — **de bain** der bun *bathroom*

 — **de transit** der tron·zeet *transit lounge*

salon m **de beauté** sa·lon der bo·tay *beauty salon*

sans son *without*
sec/sèche m/f sek/sesh *dry*
semaine f ser·men *week*
sentier m son·tyay *footpath*
service m sair·vees *service charge*
serviette f sair·vyet *briefcase • towel*
sœur f ser *sister*
soie f swa *silk*
soir m swar *evening*
soirée f swa·ray *party (night out)*
sortie f sor·tee *exit*
sortir sor·teer *go out*
sous-titres m soo·tee·trer *subtitles*
sous-vêtements m soo·vet·mon *underwear*
soutien-gorge m soo·tyung·gorzh *bra*
sparadrap m spa·ra·dra *Band-Aid*
spectacle m spek·ta·kler *show*
station f **de métro** sta·syon der may·tro *metro station*
station f **de taxi** sta·syon der tak·see *taxi stand*
station-service f sta·syon·sair·vees *petrol station*
sud m sewd *south*
supérette f **de quartier** sew·pay·ret der kar·tyay *convenience store*
supermarché m sew·pair·mar·shay *supermarket*

T

tableau m ta·blo *painting (a work)*
taie f **d'oreiller** tay do·ray·yay *pillowcase*
taille f tai *size (general)*
tailleur m ta·yer *tailor*
tante f tont *aunt*
tarif m ta·reef *fare*
taux m **de change** to der shonzh *exchange rate*
taxe f **d'aéroport** taks da·ay·ro·por *airport tax*
télécarte f tay·lay·kart *phone card*

téléphone m **portable** tay·lay·fon por·ta·bler *mobile phone*
télésiège m tay·lay·syezh *chairlift (skiing)*
timbre m tum·brer *stamp*
tôt to *early*
tout(e) m/f too(t) *everything*
traiteur m tre·ter *delicatessen*
toux f too *cough*

V

vacances f pl va·kons *holidays*
valider va·lee·day *validate*
valise f va·leez *suitcase*
vélo m vay·lo *bicycle*
vert(e) m/f vair(t) *green*
veste f vest *jacket*
vestiaire m vays·tyair *cloakroom*
vêtements m pl vet·mon *clothing*
viande f vyond *meat*
ville f veel *city*
vin m vun *wine*
visite f **guidée** vee·zeet gee·day *guided tour*
voie de terre vwa der tair *surface mail (land)*
voie maritime vwa ma·ree·teem *surface mail (sea)*
voiture f vwa·tewr *car*
vol m vol *flight*
volé(e) m/f vo·lay *stolen*
voyage m vwa·yazh *tour*
— **d'affaires** da·fair *business trip*
voyageur/voyageuse m/f vwa·ya·zher/ vwa·ya·zherz *passenger*
vue f vew *view*

W

wagon-lit m va·gon·lee *sleeping car*
wagon-restaurant m va·gon·res·to·ron *dining car*

LOOK UP

A

B

C

D

E

What kind of traveller are you?

A. You're eating chicken for dinner *again* because it's the only word you know.

B. When no one understands what you say, you step closer and shout louder.

C. When the barman doesn't understand your order, you point frantically at the beer.

D. You're surrounded by locals, swapping jokes, email addresses and experiences – other travellers want to borrow your phrasebook.

If you answered A, B, or C, you NEED Lonely Planet's phrasebooks.

- **Talk to everyone everywhere**
  Over 120 languages, more than any other publisher
- **The right words at the right time**
  Quick-reference colour sections, two-way dictionary, easy pronunciation, every possible subject
- **Lonely Planet Fast Talk** – essential language for short trips and weekends away
- **Lonely Planet Phrasebooks** – for every phrase you need in every language you want

'Best for curious and independent travellers' – Wall Street Journal

Lonely Planet Offices

Australia
90 Maribyrnong St, Footscray,
Victoria 3011
☎ 03 8379 8000
fax 03 8379 8111
email: talk2us@lonelyplanet.com.au

USA
150 Linden St, Oakland,
CA 94607
☎ 510 893 8555
fax 510 893 8572
email: info@lonelyplanet.com

UK
72-82 Rosebery Ave,
London EC1R 4RW
☎ 020 7841 9000
fax 020 7841 9001
email: go@lonelyplanet.co.uk

www.lonelyplanet.com